THE MAJOR PROPHETS

BOOK 2

BIBLE STUDY GUIDES AND COPYWORK BOOK

Isaiah, Jeremiah, Lamentations, Ezekiel, and Daniel

MEMORIZE THE BIBLE

BIBLE COPYWORKS

Copyright 2016

HOW TO USE THIS BOOK

The living Bible is the guide to everyday life. As a believer in the oneness of God's magnificence, reading and meditating on the words of the Bible will help you. But what actions could you take to better your understanding of God's words? What methods could you employ that could broaden your understanding of your place in the world? What method could you use to assist you in understanding the Bible's awesome wisdom? How can you memorize the most relevant passages that will help guide you on the straight path? How can you hold your love of God deeply in your heart?

Embracing the auspicious work of transcribing the Bible is the answer to these questions. And Bible Copyworks provides you with the perfect workbooks to accomplish this "must do" activity.

There is a total of fourteen Bible Study Guides and Copywork workbooks available as part of the Bible Copywork series. Completing the copywork available to you in each title will enable you to more deeply contemplate and come to a fuller understanding of the Bible. The dedicated scribe (you), will never fail to praise God, strengthen the just, confirm the good, and confound the proud.

But let's keep this simple, the act of transcribing the words of God will transform your life – you will never be the same. Your devotion will be an act of meditation and prayer. Your heart will be full of God's love.

In many ways, it doesn't matter which Bible Copyworks title you start with. But if you are like many, you will start at the beginning. To help keep track of the order of the titles and your progress, here is a listing of the titles:

01-The Pentateuch BOOK 1	08-The Major Prophets BOOK 1
02-The Pentateuch BOOK 2	09-The Major Prophets BOOK 2
03-The Historical Books BOOK 1	10-The Minor Prophets
04-The Historical Books BOOK 2	11-The Gospels and Acts BOOK 1
05-The Historical Books BOOK 3	12-The Gospels and Acts BOOK 2
06-The Poetic and Wisdom Writings BOOK 1	13-Paul's Epistles and Hebrews
07-The Poetic and Wisdom Writings BOOK 2	14 - General Epistles and the Apocalypse

On a parting note, the best way to use this book is to be in the right frame of mind. Here is a wonderful prayer to help –

My dear God, I ask not for more riches, but for more wisdom with which to make wiser use of the gift you gave me at birth, that is, the power to control my own mind to whatever ends you desire of me. My God, please never forget me, remind me daily of my purpose and mission in this life. Let me please you. Let me deeply understand your words. Amen.

Always remember –

Ephesians 5:17

"We should not be unwise, but understand what God's will is. So, God has a will for our lives, and He expects us to learn what that will is."

TABLE OF CONTENT

THE BOOK OF THE PROPHET
EZEKIEL

EZEKIEL

CHAPTER 1

1 Now it came to pass in the thirtieth year, in the fourth month, in the fifth day of the month, as I was among the captives by the river of Chebar, that the heavens were opened, and I saw visions of God.

2 In the fifth day of the month, which was the fifth year of king Jehoiachin's captivity,

3 The word of the LORD came expressly unto Ezekiel the priest, the son of Buzi, in the land of the Chaldeans by the river Chebar; and the hand of the LORD was there upon him.

4 And I looked, and, behold, a whirlwind came out of the north, a great cloud, and a fire infolding itself, and a brightness was about it, and out of the midst thereof as the colour of amber, out of the midst of the fire.

5 Also out of the midst thereof came the likeness of four living creatures. And this was their appearance; they had the likeness of a man.

6 And every one had four faces, and every one had four wings.

EZEKIEL

7 And their feet were straight feet; and the sole of their feet was like the sole of a calf's foot: and they sparkled like the colour of burnished brass.

8 And they had the hands of a man under their wings on their four sides; and they four had their faces and their wings.

9 Their wings were joined one to another; they turned not when they went; they went every one straight forward.

10 As for the likeness of their faces, they four had the face of a man, and the face of a lion, on the right side: and they four had the face of an ox on the left side; they four also had the face of an eagle.

11 Thus were their faces: and their wings were stretched upward; two wings of every one were joined one to another, and two covered their bodies.

12 And they went every one straight forward: whither the spirit was to go, they went; and they turned not when they went.

EZEKIEL

13 As for the likeness of the living creatures, their appearance was like burning coals of fire, and like the appearance of lamps: it went up and down among the living creatures; and the fire was bright, and out of the fire went forth lightning.

14 And the living creatures ran and returned as the appearance of a flash of lightning.

15 Now as I beheld the living creatures, behold one wheel upon the earth by the living creatures, with his four faces.

16 The appearance of the wheels and their work was like unto the colour of a beryl: and they four had one likeness: and their appearance and their work was as it were a wheel in the middle of a wheel.

17 When they went, they went upon their four sides: and they turned not when they went.

18 As for their rings, they were so high that they were dreadful; and their rings were full of eyes round about them four.

EZEKIEL

19 And when the living creatures went, the wheels went by them: and when the living creatures were lifted up from the earth, the wheels were lifted up.

20 Whithersoever the spirit was to go, they went, thither was their spirit to go; and the wheels were lifted up over against them: for the spirit of the living creature was in the wheels.

21 When those went, these went; and when those stood, these stood; and when those were lifted up from the earth, the wheels were lifted up over against them: for the spirit of the living creature was in the wheels.

22 And the likeness of the firmament upon the heads of the living creature was as the colour of the terrible crystal, stretched forth over their heads above.

23 And under the firmament were their wings straight, the one toward the other: every one had two, which covered on this side, and every one had two, which covered on that side, their bodies.

24 And when they went, I heard the noise of their wings, like the noise of great waters, as the voice of the Almighty, the voice of speech, as the noise of an host: when they stood, they let down their wings.

25 And there was a voice from the firmament that was over their heads, when they stood, and had let down their wings.

26 And above the firmament that was over their heads was the likeness of a throne, as the appearance of a sapphire stone: and upon the likeness of the throne was the likeness as the appearance of a man above upon it.

27 And I saw as the colour of amber, as the appearance of fire round about within it, from the appearance of his loins even upward, and from the appearance of his loins even downward, I saw as it were the appearance of fire, and it had brightness round about.

28 As the appearance of the bow that is in the cloud in the day of rain, so was the appearance of the brightness round about. This was the appearance of the likeness of the glory of the LORD. And when I saw it, I fell upon my face, and I heard a voice of one that spake.

CHAPTER 2

1 And he said unto me, Son of man, stand upon thy feet, and I will speak unto thee.

2 And the spirit entered into me when he spake unto me, and set me upon my feet, that I heard him that spake unto me.

3 And he said unto me, Son of man, I send thee to the children of Israel, to a rebellious nation that hath rebelled against me: they and their fathers have transgressed against me, even unto this very day.

4 For they are impudent children and stiffhearted. I do send thee unto them; and thou shalt say unto them, Thus saith the Lord GOD.

EZEKIEL

5 - And they, whether they will hear, or whether they will forbear, (for they are a rebellious house,) yet shall know that there hath been a prophet among them.

6 - And thou, son of man, be not afraid of them, neither be afraid of their words, though briers and thorns be with thee, and thou dost dwell among scorpions: be not afraid of their words, nor be dismayed at their looks, though they be a rebellious house.

7 - And thou shalt speak my words unto them, whether they will hear, or whether they will forbear: for they are most rebellious.

8 - But thou, son of man, hear what I say unto thee; Be not thou rebellious like that rebellious house: open thy mouth, and eat that I give thee.

9 - And when I looked, behold, an hand was sent unto me; and, lo, a roll of a book was therein;

10 - And he spread it before me; and it was written within and without: and there was written therein lamentations, and mourning, and woe.

CHAPTER 3

1 Moreover he said unto me, Son of man, eat that thou findest; eat this roll, and go speak unto the house of Israel.

2 So I opened my mouth, and he caused me to eat that roll.

3 And he said unto me, Son of man, cause thy belly to eat, and fill thy bowels with this roll that I give thee. Then did I eat it; and it was in my mouth as honey for sweetness.

4 And he said unto me, Son of man, go, get thee unto the house of Israel, and speak with my words unto them.

5 For thou art not sent to a people of a strange speech and of an hard language, but to the house of Israel.

6 Not to many people of a strange speech and of an hard language, whose words thou canst not understand. Surely, had I sent thee to them, they would have hearkened unto thee.

EZEKIEL

7 But the house of Israel will not hearken unto thee;
for they will not hearken unto me: for all the house of
Israel are impudent and hardhearted.

8 Behold, I have made thy face strong against their
faces, and thy forehead strong against their
foreheads.

9 As an adamant harder than flint have I made thy
forehead: fear them not, neither be dismayed at their
looks, though they be a rebellious house.

10 Moreover he said unto me, Son of man, all my
words that I shall speak unto thee receive in thine
heart, and hear with thine ears.

11 And go, get thee to them of the captivity, unto the
children of thy people, and speak unto them, and tell
them, Thus saith the Lord GOD; whether they will
hear, or whether they will forbear.

12 Then the spirit took me up, and I heard behind me
a voice of a great rushing, saying, Blessed be the
glory of the LORD from his place.

EZEKIEL

13 I heard also the noise of the wings of the living creatures that touched one another, and the noise of the wheels over against them, and a noise of a great rushing.

14 So the spirit lifted me up, and took me away, and I went in bitterness, in the heat of my spirit; but the hand of the LORD was strong upon me.

15 Then I came to them of the captivity at Tel-abib, that dwelt by the river of Chebar, and I sat where they sat, and remained there astonished among them seven days.

16 And it came to pass at the end of seven days, that the word of the LORD came unto me, saying,

17 Son of man, I have made thee a watchman unto the house of Israel: therefore hear the word at my mouth, and give them warning from me.

18 When I say unto the wicked, Thou shalt surely die; and thou givest him not warning, nor speakest to warn the wicked from his wicked way, to save his life; the same wicked man shall die in his iniquity; but his blood will I require at thine hand.

EZEKIEL

19 Yet if thou warn the wicked, and he turn not from his wickedness, nor from his wicked way, he shall die in his iniquity; but thou hast delivered thy soul.

20 Again, When a righteous man doth turn from his righteousness, and commit iniquity, and I lay a stumblingblock before him, he shall die: because thou hast not given him warning, he shall die in his sin, and his righteousness which he hath done shall not be remembered; but his blood will I require at thine hand.

21 Nevertheless if thou warn the righteous man, that the righteous sin not, and he doth not sin, he shall surely live, because he is warned; also thou hast delivered thy soul.

22 And the hand of the LORD was there upon me; and he said unto me, Arise, go forth into the plain, and I will there talk with thee.

23 Then I arose, and went forth into the plain: and, behold, the glory of the LORD stood there, as the glory which I saw by the river of Chebar: and I fell on my face.

2:4 Then the spirit entered into me, and set me upon my feet, and spake with me, and said unto me, Go, shut thyself within thine house.

2:5 But thou, O son of man, behold, they shall put bands upon thee, and shall bind thee with them, and thou shalt not go out among them.

2:6 And I will make thy tongue cleave to the roof of thy mouth, that thou shalt be dumb, and shalt not be to them a reprover: for they are a rebellious house.

2:7 But when I speak with thee, I will open thy mouth, and thou shalt say unto them, Thus saith the Lord GOD; He that heareth, let him hear; and he that forbeareth, let him forbear: for they are a rebellious house.

CHAPTER 4

1 Thou also, son of man, take thee a tile, and lay it before thee, and pourtray upon it the city, even Jerusalem:

EZEKIEL

2 And lay siege against it, and build a fort against it,
and cast a mount against it set the camp also against
it, and set battering rams against it round about.

3 Moreover take thou unto thee an iron pan, and set
it for a wall of iron between thee and the city: and set
thy face against it, and it shall be besieged, and thou
shalt lay siege against it. This shall be a sign to the
house of Israel.

4 Lie thou also upon thy left side, and lay the iniquity
of the house of Israel upon it according to the
number of the days that thou shalt lie upon it thou
shalt bear their iniquity.

5 For I have laid upon thee the years of their iniquity,
according to the number of the days, three hundred
and ninety days: so shalt thou bear the iniquity of the
house of Israel.

6 And when thou hast accomplished them, lie again
on thy right side, and thou shalt bear the iniquity of
the house of Judah forty days: I have appointed thee
each day for a year.

EZEKIEL

7 Therefore thou shalt set thy face toward the siege of Jerusalem, and thine arm shall be uncovered, and thou shalt prophesy against it.

8 And behold, I will lay bands upon thee, and thou shalt not turn thee from one side to another, till thou hast ended the days of thy siege.

9 Take thou also unto thee wheat, and barley, and beans, and lentiles, and millet, and fitches, and put them in one vessel, and make thee bread thereof, according to the number of the days that thou shalt lie upon thy side, three hundred and ninety days shalt thou eat thereof.

10 And thy meat which thou shalt eat shall be by weight, twenty shekels a day: from time to time shalt thou eat it.

11 Thou shalt drink also water by measure, the sixth part of an hin: from time to time shalt thou drink.

12 And thou shalt eat it as barley cakes, and thou shalt bake it with dung that cometh out of man, in their sight.

EZEKIEL

13 And the LORD said, Even thus shall the children of Israel eat their defiled bread among the Gentiles, whither I will drive them.

14 Then said I, Ah Lord GOD! behold, my soul hath not been polluted: for from my youth up even till now have I not eaten of that which dieth of itself, or is torn in pieces; neither came there abominable flesh into my mouth.

15 Then he said unto me, Lo, I have given thee cow's dung for man's dung, and thou shalt prepare thy bread therewith.

16 Moreover he said unto me, Son of man, behold, I will break the staff of bread in Jerusalem: and they shall eat bread by weight, and with care; and they shall drink water by measure, and with astonishment:

17 That they may want bread and water, and be astonied one with another, and consume away for their iniquity.

CHAPTER 5

1 And thou, son of man, take thee a sharp knife, take thee a barber's razor, and cause it to pass upon thine head and upon thy beard: then take thee balances to weigh, and divide the hair.

2 Thou shalt burn with fire a third part in the midst of the city, when the days of the siege are fulfilled: and thou shalt take a third part, and smite about it with a knife: and a third part thou shalt scatter in the wind; and I will draw out a sword after them.

3 Thou shalt also take thereof a few in number, and bind them in thy skirts.

4 Then take of them again, and cast them into the midst of the fire, and burn them in the fire; for thereof shall a fire come forth into all the house of Israel.

5 Thus saith the Lord GOD; This is Jerusalem: I have set it in the midst of the nations and countries that are round about her.

6 And she hath changed my judgments into
wickedness more than the nations, and my statutes
more than the countries that are round about her: for
they have refused my judgments and my statutes,
they have not walked in them.

7 Therefore thus saith the Lord GOD; Because ye
multiplied more than the nations that are round about
you, and have not walked in my statutes, neither have
kept my judgments, neither have done according to
the judgments of the nations that are round about
you;

8 Therefore thus saith the Lord GOD; Behold, I,
even I, am against thee, and will execute judgments in
the midst of thee in the sight of the nations.

9 And I will do in thee that which I have not done,
and whereunto I will not do any more the like, because
of all thine abominations.

10 Therefore the fathers shall eat the sons in the
midst of thee, and the sons shall eat their fathers; and
I will execute judgments in thee, and the whole
remnant of thee will I scatter into all the winds.

EZEKIEL

11 Wherefore, as I live, saith the Lord GOD; Surely, because thou hast defiled my sanctuary with all thy detestable things, and with all thine abominations, therefore will I also diminish thee; neither shall mine eye spare, neither will I have any pity.

12 A third part of thee shall die with the pestilence, and with famine shall they be consumed in the midst of thee: and a third part shall fall by the sword round about thee; and I will scatter a third part into all the winds, and I will draw out a sword after them.

13 Thus shall mine anger be accomplished, and I will cause my fury to rest upon them, and I will be comforted: and they shall know that I the LORD have spoken it in my zeal, when I have accomplished my fury in them.

14 Moreover I will make thee waste, and a reproach among the nations that are round about thee, in the sight of all that pass by.

EZEKIEL

15 So it shall be a reproach and a taunt, an instruction and an astonishment unto the nations that are round about thee, when I shall execute judgments in thee in anger and in fury and in furious rebukes. I the LORD have spoken it.

16 When I shall send upon them the evil arrows of famine, which shall be for their destruction, and which I will send to destroy you: and I will increase the famine upon you, and will break your staff of bread:

17 So will I send upon you famine and evil beasts, and they shall bereave thee; and pestilence and blood shall pass through thee; and I will bring the sword upon thee. I the LORD have spoken it.

CHAPTER 6

1 And the word of the LORD came unto me, saying,

2 Son of man, set thy face toward the mountains of Israel, and prophesy against them,

EZEKIEL

3 And say, Ye mountains of Israel, hear the word of the Lord GOD; Thus saith the Lord GOD to the mountains, and to the hills, to the rivers, and to the valleys; Behold, I, even I, will bring a sword upon you, and I will destroy your high places.

4 And your altars shall be desolate, and your images shall be broken: and I will cast down your slain men before your idols.

5 And I will lay the dead carcases of the children of Israel before their idols; and I will scatter your bones round about your altars.

6 In all your dwellingplaces the cities shall be laid waste, and the high places shall be desolate; that your altars may be laid waste and made desolate, and your idols may be broken and cease, and your images may be cut down, and your works may be abolished.

7 And the slain shall fall in the midst of you, and ye shall know that I am the LORD.

8 Yet will I leave a remnant, that ye may have some that shall escape the sword among the nations, when ye shall be scattered through the countries.

EZEKIEL

9 - And they that escape of you shall remember me among the nations whither they shall be carried captives, because I am broken with their whorish heart, which hath departed from me, and with their eyes, which go a whoring after their idols: and they shall lothe themselves for the evils which they have committed in all their abominations.

10 - And they shall know that I am the LORD, and that I have not said in vain that I would do this evil unto them.

11 - Thus saith the Lord GOD; Smite with thine hand, and stamp with thy foot, and say, Alas for all the evil abominations of the house of Israel! for they shall fall by the sword, by the famine, and by the pestilence.

12 - He that is far off shall die of the pestilence; and he that is near shall fall by the sword; and he that remaineth and is besieged shall die by the famine: thus will I accomplish my fury upon them.

13 Then shall ye know that I am the LORD, when their slain men shall be among their idols round about their altars, upon every high hill, in all the tops of the mountains, and under every green tree, and under every thick oak, the place where they did offer sweet savour to all their idols.

14 So will I stretch out my hand upon them, and make the land desolate, yea, more desolate than the wilderness toward Diblath, in all their habitations: and they shall know that I am the LORD.

CHAPTER 7

1 Moreover the word of the LORD came unto me, saying,

2 Also, thou son of man, thus saith the Lord GOD unto the land of Israel; An end, the end is come upon the four corners of the land.

3 Now is the end come upon thee, and I will send mine anger upon thee, and will judge thee according to thy ways, and will recompense upon thee all thine abominations.

EZEKIEL

4 And mine eye shall not spare thee, neither will I
have pity: but I will recompense thy ways upon thee,
and thine abominations shall be in the midst of thee:
and ye shall know that I am the LORD.

5 Thus saith the Lord GOD; An evil, an only evil,
behold, is come.

6 An end is come, the end is come: it watcheth for
thee; behold, it is come.

7 The morning is come unto thee, O thou that
dwellest in the land: the time is come, the day of
trouble is near, and not the sounding again of the
mountains.

8 Now will I shortly pour out my fury upon thee, and
accomplish mine anger upon thee: and I will judge
thee according to thy ways, and will recompense thee
for all thine abominations.

9 And mine eye shall not spare, neither will I have
pity: I will recompense thee according to thy ways and
thine abominations that are in the midst of thee; and
ye shall know that I am the LORD that smiteth.

EZEKIEL

10 Behold the day, behold, it is come: the morning is gone forth; the rod hath blossomed, pride hath budded.

11 Violence is risen up into a rod of wickedness: none of them shall remain, nor of their multitude, nor of any of theirs: neither shall there be wailing for them.

12 The time is come, the day draweth near: let not the buyer rejoice, nor the seller mourn: for wrath is upon all the multitude thereof.

13 For the seller shall not return to that which is sold, although they were yet alive: for the vision is touching the whole multitude thereof, which shall not return; neither shall any strengthen himself in the iniquity of his life.

14 They have blown the trumpet, even to make all ready; but none goeth to the battle: for my wrath is upon all the multitude thereof.

15 The sword is without, and the pestilence and the famine within: he that is in the field shall die with the sword; and he that is in the city, famine and pestilence shall devour him.

EZEKIEL

16 But they that escape of them shall escape, and shall be on the mountains like doves of the valleys, all of them mourning, every one for his iniquity.

17 All hands shall be feeble, and all knees shall be weak as water.

18 They shall also gird themselves with sackcloth, and horror shall cover them; and shame shall be upon all faces, and baldness upon all their heads.

19 They shall cast their silver in the streets, and their gold shall be removed: their silver and their gold shall not be able to deliver them in the day of the wrath of the LORD: they shall not satisfy their souls, neither fill their bowels: because it is the stumblingblock of their iniquity.

20 As for the beauty of his ornament, he set it in majesty: but they made the images of their abominations and of their detestable things therein: therefore have I set it far from them.

21 And I will give it into the hands of the strangers for a prey, and to the wicked of the earth for a spoil; and they shall pollute it.

EZEKIEL

2:2- My face will I turn also from them, and they shall pollute my secret place: for the robbers shall enter into it, and defile it.

2:3- Make a chain: for the land is full of bloody crimes, and the city is full of violence.

2:4- Wherefore I will bring the worst of the heathen, and they shall possess their houses: I will also make the pomp of the strong to cease; and their holy places shall be defiled.

2:5- Destruction cometh; and they shall seek peace, and there shall be none.

2:6- Mischief shall come upon mischief, and rumour shall be upon rumour; then shall they seek a vision of the prophet; but the law shall perish from the priest, and counsel from the ancients.

2:7- The king shall mourn, and the prince shall be clothed with desolation, and the hands of the people of the land shall be troubled: I will do unto them after their way, and according to their deserts will I judge them; and they shall know that I am the LORD.

EZEKIEL

CHAPTER 8

1 And it came to pass in the sixth year, in the sixth month, in the fifth day of the month, as I sat in mine house, and the elders of Judah sat before me, that the hand of the Lord GOD fell there upon me.

2 Then I beheld, and lo a likeness as the appearance of fire: from the appearance of his loins even downward, fire; and from his loins even upward, as the appearance of brightness, as the colour of amber.

3 And he put forth the form of an hand, and took me by a lock of mine head; and the spirit lifted me up between the earth and the heaven, and brought me in the visions of God to Jerusalem, to the door of the inner gate that looketh toward the north; where was the seat of the image of jealousy, which provoketh to jealousy.

4 And, behold, the glory of the God of Israel was there, according to the vision that I saw in the plain.

EZEKIEL

5 Then said he unto me, Son of man, lift up thine eyes now the way toward the north. So I lifted up mine eyes the way toward the north, and behold northward at the gate of the altar this image of jealousy in the entry.

6 He said furthermore unto me, Son of man, seest thou what they do? even the great abominations that the house of Israel committeth here, that I should go far off from my sanctuary? but turn thee yet again, and thou shalt see greater abominations.

7 And he brought me to the door of the court; and when I looked, behold a hole in the wall.

8 Then said he unto me, Son of man, dig now in the wall: and when I had digged in the wall, behold a door.

9 And he said unto me, Go in, and behold the wicked abominations that they do here.

10 So I went in and saw; and behold every form of creeping things, and abominable beasts, and all the idols of the house of Israel, pourtrayed upon the wall round about.

EZEKIEL

11 And there stood before them seventy men of the ancients of the house of Israel, and in the midst of them stood Jaazaniah the son of Shaphan, with every man his censer in his hand; and a thick cloud of incense went up.

12 Then said he unto me, Son of man, hast thou seen what the ancients of the house of Israel do in the dark, every man in the chambers of his imagery? for they say, The LORD seeth us not; the LORD hath forsaken the earth.

13 He said also unto me, Turn thee yet again, and thou shalt see greater abominations that they do.

14 Then he brought me to the door of the gate of the LORD'S house which was toward the north; and, behold, there sat women weeping for Tammuz.

15 Then said he unto me, Hast thou seen this, O son of man? turn thee yet again, and thou shalt see greater abominations than these.

16 And he brought me into the inner court of the LORD'S house, and behold, at the door of the temple of the LORD, between the porch and the altar, were about five and twenty men, with their backs toward the temple of the LORD, and their faces toward the east; and they worshipped the sun toward the east.

17 Then he said unto me, Hast thou seen this, O son of man? Is it a light thing to the house of Judah that they commit the abominations which they commit here? for they have filled the land with violence, and have returned to provoke me to anger: and, lo, they put the branch to their nose.

18 Therefore will I also deal in fury: mine eye shall not spare, neither will I have pity: and though they cry in mine ears with a loud voice, yet will I not hear them.

CHAPTER 9

1 He cried also in mine ears with a loud voice, saying, Cause them that have charge over the city to draw near, even every man with his destroying weapon in his hand.

EZEKIEL

2 And, behold, six men came from the way of the higher gate, which lieth toward the north, and every man a slaughter weapon in his hand; and one man among them was clothed with linen, with a writer's inkhorn by his side: and they went in, and stood beside the brasen altar.

3 And the glory of the God of Israel was gone up from the cherub, whereupon he was, to the threshold of the house. And he called to the man clothed with linen, which had the writer's inkhorn by his side;

4 And the LORD said unto him, Go through the midst of the city, through the midst of Jerusalem, and set a mark upon the foreheads of the men that sigh and that cry for all the abominations that be done in the midst thereof.

5 And to the others he said in mine hearing, Go ye after him through the city, and smite: let not your eye spare, neither have ye pity:

37

6 Slay utterly old and young, both maids, and little
children, and women: but come not near any man upon
whom is the mark; and begin at my sanctuary. Then
they began at the ancient men which were before the
house.

7 And he said unto them, Defile the house, and fill the
courts with the slain: go ye forth. And they went forth,
and slew in the city.

8 And it came to pass, while they were slaying them,
and I was left, that I fell upon my face, and cried, and
said, Ah Lord GOD! wilt thou destroy all the residue
of Israel in thy pouring out of thy fury upon
Jerusalem?

9 Then said he unto me, The iniquity of the house of
Israel and Judah is exceeding great, and the land is
full of blood, and the city full of perverseness: for they
say, The LORD hath forsaken the earth, and the
LORD seeth not.

10 And as for me also, mine eye shall not spare,
neither will I have pity, but I will recompense their way
upon their head.

EZEKIEL

11 And, behold, the man clothed with linen, which had the inkhorn by his side, reported the matter, saying, I have done as thou hast commanded me.

CHAPTER 10

1 Then I looked, and, behold, in the firmament that was above the head of the cherubims there appeared over them as it were a sapphire stone, as the appearance of the likeness of a throne.

2 And he spake unto the man clothed with linen, and said, Go in between the wheels, even under the cherub, and fill thine hand with coals of fire from between the cherubims, and scatter them over the city. And he went in in my sight.

3 Now the cherubims stood on the right side of the house, when the man went in; and the cloud filled the inner court.

4 Then the glory of the LORD went up from the cherub, and stood over the threshold of the house; and the house was filled with the cloud, and the court was full of the brightness of the LORD'S glory.

EZEKIEL

5 And the sound of the cherubims' wings was heard even to the outer court, as the voice of the Almighty God when he speaketh.

6 And it came to pass, that when he had commanded the man clothed with linen, saying, Take fire from between the wheels, from between the cherubims; then he went in, and stood beside the wheels.

7 And one cherub stretched forth his hand from between the cherubims unto the fire that was between the cherubims, and took thereof, and put it into the hands of him that was clothed with linen: who took it, and went out.

8 And there appeared in the cherubims the form of a man's hand under their wings.

9 And when I looked, behold the four wheels by the cherubims, one wheel by one cherub, and another wheel by another cherub: and the appearance of the wheels was as the colour of a beryl stone.

10 And as for their appearances, they four had one likeness, as if a wheel had been in the midst of a wheel.

EZEKIEL

1 When they went, they went upon their four sides; they turned not as they went, but to the place whither the head looked they followed it; they turned not as they went.

2 And their whole body, and their backs, and their hands, and their wings, and the wheels, were full of eyes round about, even the wheels that they four had.

3 As for the wheels, it was cried unto them in my hearing, O wheel.

4 And every one had four faces: the first face was the face of a cherub, and the second face was the face of a man, and the third the face of a lion, and the fourth the face of an eagle.

5 And the cherubims were lifted up. This is the living creatures that I saw by the river of Chebar.

6 And when the cherubims went, the wheels went by them: and when the cherubims lifted up their wings to mount up from the earth, the same wheels also turned not from beside them.

EZEKIEL

17 When they stood, these stood; and when they were lifted up, these lifted up themselves also: for the spirit of the living creature was in them.

18 Then the glory of the LORD departed from off the threshold of the house, and stood over the cherubims.

19 And the cherubims lifted up their wings, and mounted up from the earth in my sight: when they went out, the wheels also were beside them, and every one stood at the door of the east gate of the LORD'S house; and the glory of the God of Israel was over them above.

20 This is the living creature that I saw under the God of Israel by the river of Chebar; and I knew that they were the cherubims.

21 Every one had four faces apiece, and every one four wings; and the likeness of the hands of a man was under their wings.

EZEKIEL

22 And the likeness of their faces was the same faces which I saw by the river of Chebar, their appearances and themselves: they went every one straight forward.

CHAPTER 11

1 Moreover the spirit lifted me up, and brought me unto the east gate of the LORDS house, which looketh eastward: and behold at the door of the gate five and twenty men; among whom I saw Jaazaniah the son of Azur, and Pelatiah the son of Benaiah, princes of the people.

2 Then said he unto me, Son of man, these are the men that devise mischief, and give wicked counsel in this city:

3 Which say, It is not near; let us build houses: this city is the caldron, and we be the flesh.

4 Therefore prophesy against them, prophesy, O son of man.

EZEKIEL

5 And the Spirit of the LORD fell upon me, and said unto me, Speak; Thus saith the LORD; Thus have ye said, O house of Israel: for I know the things that come into your mind, every one of them.

6 Ye have multiplied your slain in this city, and ye have filled the streets thereof with the slain.

7 Therefore thus saith the Lord GOD; Your slain whom ye have laid in the midst of it, they are the flesh, and this city is the caldron: but I will bring you forth out of the midst of it.

8 Ye have feared the sword; and I will bring a sword upon you, saith the Lord GOD.

9 And I will bring you out of the midst thereof, and deliver you into the hands of strangers, and will execute judgments among you.

10 Ye shall fall by the sword; I will judge you in the border of Israel; and ye shall know that I am the LORD.

11 This city shall not be your caldron, neither shall ye be the flesh in the midst thereof; but I will judge you in the border of Israel:

EZEKIEL

12 And ye shall know that I am the LORD: for ye have not walked in my statutes, neither executed my judgments, but have done after the manners of the heathen that are round about you.

13 And it came to pass, when I prophesied, that Pelatiah the son of Benaiah died. Then fell I down upon my face, and cried with a loud voice, and said, Ah Lord GOD! wilt thou make a full end of the remnant of Israel?

14 Again the word of the LORD came unto me, saying,

15 Son of man, thy brethren, even thy brethren, the men of thy kindred, and all the house of Israel wholly, are they unto whom the inhabitants of Jerusalem have said, Get you far from the LORD: unto us is this land given in possession.

16 Therefore say, Thus saith the Lord GOD; Although I have cast them far off among the heathen, and although I have scattered them among the countries, yet will I be to them as a little sanctuary in the countries where they shall come.

EZEKIEL

17 Therefore say, Thus saith the Lord GOD; I will even gather you from the people, and assemble you out of the countries where ye have been scattered, and I will give you the land of Israel.

18 And they shall come thither, and they shall take away all the detestable things thereof and all the abominations thereof from thence.

19 And I will give them one heart, and I will put a new spirit within you; and I will take the stony heart out of their flesh, and will give them an heart of flesh:

20 That they may walk in my statutes, and keep mine ordinances, and do them: and they shall be my people, and I will be their God.

21 But as for them whose heart walketh after the heart of their detestable things and their abominations, I will recompense their way upon their own heads, saith the Lord GOD.

22 Then did the cherubims lift up their wings, and the wheels beside them; and the glory of the God of Israel was over them above.

EZEKIEL

23 And the glory of the LORD went up from the midst of the city, and stood upon the mountain which is on the east side of the city.

24 Afterwards the spirit took me up, and brought me in a vision by the Spirit of God into Chaldea, to them of the captivity. So the vision that I had seen went up from me.

25 Then I spake unto them of the captivity all the things that the LORD had shewed me.

CHAPTER 12

1 The word of the LORD also came unto me, saying,

2 Son of man, thou dwellest in the midst of a rebellious house, which have eyes to see, and see not; they have ears to hear, and hear not: for they are a rebellious house.

3 Therefore, thou son of man, prepare thee stuff for removing, and remove by day in their sight; and thou shalt remove from thy place to another place in their sight: it may be they will consider, though they be a rebellious house.

EZEKIEL

4 Then shalt thou bring forth thy stuff by day in their sight, as stuff for removing: and thou shalt go forth at even in their sight, as they that go forth into captivity.

5 Dig thou through the wall in their sight, and carry out thereby.

6 In their sight shalt thou bear it upon thy shoulders, and carry it forth in the twilight: thou shalt cover thy face, that thou see not the ground: for I have set thee for a sign unto the house of Israel.

7 And I did so as I was commanded: I brought forth my stuff by day, as stuff for captivity, and in the even I digged through the wall with mine hand: I brought it forth in the twilight, and I bare it upon my shoulder in their sight.

8 And in the morning came the word of the LORD unto me, saying,

9 Son of man, hath not the house of Israel, the rebellious house, said unto thee, What doest thou?

10 Say thou unto them, Thus saith the Lord GOD; This burden concerneth the prince in Jerusalem, and all the house of Israel that are among them.

EZEKIEL

1 Say, I am your sign: like as I have done, so shall it be done unto them: they shall remove and go into captivity.

2 And the prince that is among them shall bear upon his shoulder in the twilight, and shall go forth: they shall dig through the wall to carry out thereby: he shall cover his face, that he see not the ground with his eyes.

3 My net also will I spread upon him, and he shall be taken in my snare: and I will bring him to Babylon to the land of the Chaldeans; yet shall he not see it, though he shall die there.

4 And I will scatter toward every wind all that are about him to help him, and all his bands; and I will draw out the sword after them.

5 And they shall know that I am the LORD, when I shall scatter them among the nations, and disperse them in the countries.

EZEKIEL

16 But I will leave a few men of them from the sword, from the famine, and from the pestilence; that they may declare all their abominations among the heathen whither they come; and they shall know that I am the LORD.

17 Moreover the word of the LORD came to me, saying,

18 Son of man, eat thy bread with quaking, and drink thy water with trembling and with carefulness;

19 And say unto the people of the land, Thus saith the Lord GOD of the inhabitants of Jerusalem, and of the land of Israel; They shall eat their bread with carefulness, and drink their water with astonishment, that her land may be desolate from all that is therein, because of the violence of all them that dwell therein.

20 And the cities that are inhabited shall be laid waste, and the land shall be desolate; and ye shall know that I am the LORD.

21 And the word of the LORD came unto me, saying,

EZEKIEL

2:2 Son of man, what is that proverb that ye have in the land of Israel, saying, The days are prolonged, and every vision faileth?

2:3 Tell them therefore, Thus saith the Lord GOD; I will make this proverb to cease, and they shall no more use it as a proverb in Israel; but say unto them, The days are at hand, and the effect of every vision.

2:4 For there shall be no more any vain vision nor flattering divination within the house of Israel.

2:5 For I am the LORD: I will speak, and the word that I shall speak shall come to pass; it shall be no more prolonged: for in your days, O rebellious house, will I say the word, and will perform it, saith the Lord GOD.

2:6 Again the word of the LORD came to me, saying,

2:7 Son of man, behold, they of the house of Israel say, The vision that he seeth is for many days to come, and he prophesieth of the times that are far off.

EZEKIEL

2-8 Therefore say unto them, Thus saith the Lord
GOD; There shall none of my words be prolonged any
more, but the word which I have spoken shall be done,
saith the Lord GOD.

CHAPTER 13

1 And the word of the LORD came unto me, saying,
2 Son of man, prophesy against the prophets of Israel
that prophesy, and say thou unto them that prophesy
out of their own hearts, Hear ye the word of the
LORD;
3 Thus saith the Lord GOD; Woe unto the foolish
prophets, that follow their own spirit, and have seen
nothing!
4 O Israel, thy prophets are like the foxes in the
deserts.
5 Ye have not gone up into the gaps, neither made up
the hedge for the house of Israel to stand in the battle
in the day of the LORD.

EZEKIEL

6 They have seen vanity and lying divination, saying, The LORD saith: and the LORD hath not sent them: and they have made others to hope that they would confirm the word.

7 Have ye not seen a vain vision, and have ye not spoken a lying divination, whereas ye say, The LORD saith it; albeit I have not spoken?

8 Therefore thus saith the Lord GOD; Because ye have spoken vanity, and seen lies, therefore, behold, I am against you, saith the Lord GOD.

9 And mine hand shall be upon the prophets that see vanity, and that divine lies: they shall not be in the assembly of my people, neither shall they be written in the writing of the house of Israel, neither shall they enter into the land of Israel; and ye shall know that I am the Lord GOD.

10 Because, even because they have seduced my people, saying, Peace; and there was no peace; and one built up a wall, and, lo, others daubed it with untempered morter:

EZEKIEL

11 Say unto them which daub it with untempered mortar, that it shall fall: there shall be an overflowing shower; and ye, O great hailstones, shall fall; and a stormy wind shall rend it.

12 Lo, when the wall is fallen, shall it not be said unto you, Where is the daubing wherewith ye have daubed it?

13 Therefore thus saith the Lord GOD; I will even rend it with a stormy wind in my fury; and there shall be an overflowing shower in mine anger, and great hailstones in my fury to consume it.

14 So will I break down the wall that ye have daubed with untempered mortar, and bring it down to the ground, so that the foundation thereof shall be discovered, and it shall fall, and ye shall be consumed in the midst thereof: and ye shall know that I am the LORD.

15 Thus will I accomplish my wrath upon the wall, and upon them that have daubed it with untempered mortar, and will say unto you, The wall is no more, neither they that daubed it;

EZEKIEL

16 To wit, the prophets of Israel which prophesy concerning Jerusalem, and which see visions of peace for her, and there is no peace, saith the Lord GOD.

17 Likewise, thou son of man, set thy face against the daughters of thy people, which prophesy out of their own heart; and prophesy thou against them,

18 And say, Thus saith the Lord GOD; Woe to the women that sew pillows to all armholes, and make kerchiefs upon the head of every stature to hunt souls! Will ye hunt the souls of my people, and will ye save the souls alive that come unto you?

19 And will ye pollute me among my people for handfuls of barley and for pieces of bread, to slay the souls that should not die, and to save the souls alive that should not live, by your lying to my people that hear your lies?

20 Wherefore thus saith the Lord GOD; Behold, I am against your pillows, wherewith ye there hunt the souls to make them fly, and I will tear them from your arms, and will let the souls go, even the souls that ye hunt to make them fly.

EZEKIEL

21 Your kerchiefs also will I tear, and deliver my people out of your hand, and they shall be no more in your hand to be hunted; and ye shall know that I am the LORD.

22 Because with lies ye have made the heart of the righteous sad, whom I have not made sad; and strengthened the hands of the wicked, that he should not return from his wicked way, by promising him life:

23 Therefore ye shall see no more vanity, nor divine divinations: for I will deliver my people out of your hand: and ye shall know that I am the LORD.

CHAPTER 14

1 Then came certain of the elders of Israel unto me, and sat before me.

2 And the word of the LORD came unto me, saying,

3 Son of man, these men have set up their idols in their heart, and put the stumblingblock of their iniquity before their face: should I be enquired of at all by them?

EZEKIEL

4 Therefore speak unto them, and say unto them, Thus saith the Lord GOD; Every man of the house of Israel that setteth up his idols in his heart, and putteth the stumblingblock of his iniquity before his face, and cometh to the prophet; I the LORD will answer him that cometh according to the multitude of his idols;

5 That I may take the house of Israel in their own heart, because they are all estranged from me through their idols.

6 Therefore say unto the house of Israel, Thus saith the Lord GOD; Repent, and turn yourselves from your idols; and turn away your faces from all your abominations.

7 For every one of the house of Israel, or of the stranger that sojourneth in Israel, which separateth himself from me, and setteth up his idols in his heart, and putteth the stumblingblock of his iniquity before his face, and cometh to a prophet to enquire of him concerning me; I the LORD will answer him by myself:

EZEKIEL

8 - And I will set my face against that man, and will make him a sign and a proverb, and I will cut him off from the midst of my people; and ye shall know that I am the LORD.

9 - And if the prophet be deceived when he hath spoken a thing, I the LORD have deceived that prophet, and I will stretch out my hand upon him, and will destroy him from the midst of my people Israel.

10 - And they shall bear the punishment of their iniquity: the punishment of the prophet shall be even as the punishment of him that seeketh unto him;

11 - That the house of Israel may go no more astray from me, neither be polluted any more with all their transgressions; but that they may be my people, and I may be their God, saith the Lord GOD.

12 - The word of the LORD came again to me, saying,

EZEKIEL

13 Son of man, when the land sinneth against me by trespassing grievously, then will I stretch out mine hand upon it, and will break the staff of the bread thereof, and will send famine upon it, and will cut off man and beast from it:

14 Though these three men, Noah, Daniel, and Job, were in it, they should deliver but their own souls by their righteousness, saith the Lord GOD.

15 If I cause noisome beasts to pass through the land, and they spoil it, so that it be desolate, that no man may pass through because of the beasts:

16 Though these three men were in it, as I live, saith the Lord GOD, they shall deliver neither sons nor daughters; they only shall be delivered, but the land shall be desolate.

17 Or if I bring a sword upon that land, and say, Sword, go through the land; so that I cut off man and beast from it:

18 Though these three men were in it, as I live, saith the Lord GOD, they shall deliver neither sons nor daughters, but they only shall be delivered themselves.

EZEKIEL

19 - Or if I send a pestilence into that land, and pour out my fury upon it in blood, to cut off from it man and beast:

20 - Though Noah, Daniel, and Job, were in it, as I live, saith the Lord GOD, they shall deliver neither son nor daughter; they shall but deliver their own souls by their righteousness.

21 For thus saith the Lord GOD; How much more when I send my four sore judgments upon Jerusalem, the sword, and the famine, and the noisome beast, and the pestilence, to cut off from it man and beast?

22 - Yet, behold, therein shall be left a remnant that shall be brought forth, both sons and daughters: behold, they shall come forth unto you, and ye shall see their way and their doings: and ye shall be comforted concerning the evil that I have brought upon Jerusalem, even concerning all that I have brought upon it.

23 And they shall comfort you, when ye see their ways and their doings: and ye shall know that I have not done without cause all that I have done in it, saith the Lord GOD.

CHAPTER 15

1 And the word of the LORD came unto me, saying,

2 Son of man, What is the vine tree more than any tree, or than a branch which is among the trees of the forest?

3 Shall wood be taken thereof to do any work? or will man take a pin of it to hang any vessel thereon?

4 Behold, it is cast into the fire for fuel; the fire devoureth both the ends of it, and the midst of it is burned. Is it meet for any work?

5 Behold, when it was whole, it was meet for no work: how much less shall it be meet yet for any work, when the fire hath devoured it, and it is burned?

EZEKIEL

6 Therefore thus saith the Lord GOD; As the vine tree among the trees of the forest, which I have given to the fire for fuel, so will I give the inhabitants of Jerusalem.

7 And I will set my face against them; they shall go out from one fire, and another fire shall devour them; and ye shall know that I am the LORD, when I set my face against them.

8 And I will make the land desolate, because they have committed a trespass, saith the Lord GOD.

CHAPTER 16

1 Again the word of the LORD came unto me, saying,

2 Son of man, cause Jerusalem to know her abominations,

3 And say, Thus saith the Lord GOD unto Jerusalem; Thy birth and thy nativity is of the land of Canaan; thy father was an Amorite, and thy mother an Hittite.

EZEKIEL

4 And as for thy nativity, in the day thou wast born thy navel was not cut, neither wast thou washed in water to supple thee; thou wast not salted at all, nor swaddled at all.

5 None eye pitied thee, to do any of these unto thee, to have compassion upon thee; but thou wast cast out in the open field, to the lothing of thy person, in the day that thou wast born.

6 And when I passed by thee, and saw thee polluted in thine own blood, I said unto thee when thou wast in thy blood, Live; yea, I said unto thee when thou wast in thy blood, Live.

7 I have caused thee to multiply as the bud of the field, and thou hast increased and waxen great, and thou art come to excellent ornaments: thy breasts are fashioned, and thine hair is grown, whereas thou wast naked and bare.

EZEKIEL

8 Now when I passed by thee, and looked upon thee, behold, thy time was the time of love; and I spread my skirt over thee, and covered thy nakedness: yea, I sware unto thee, and entered into a covenant with thee, saith the Lord GOD, and thou becamest mine.

9 Then washed I thee with water; yea, I throughly washed away thy blood from thee, and I anointed thee with oil.

10 I clothed thee also with broidered work, and shod thee with badgers' skin, and I girded thee about with fine linen, and I covered thee with silk.

11 I decked thee also with ornaments, and I put bracelets upon thy hands, and a chain on thy neck.

12 And I put a jewel on thy forehead, and earrings in thine ears, and a beautiful crown upon thine head.

13 Thus wast thou decked with gold and silver; and thy raiment was of fine linen, and silk, and broidered work; thou didst eat fine flour, and honey, and oil: and thou wast exceeding beautiful, and thou didst prosper into a kingdom.

EZEKIEL

14 And thy renown went forth among the heathen for thy beauty: for it was perfect through my comeliness, which I had put upon thee, saith the Lord GOD.

15 But thou didst trust in thine own beauty, and playedst the harlot because of thy renown, and pouredst out thy fornications on every one that passed by; his it was.

16 And of thy garments thou didst take, and deckedst thy high places with divers colours, and playedst the harlot thereupon: the like things shall not come, neither shall it be so.

17 Thou hast also taken thy fair jewels of my gold and of my silver, which I had given thee, and madest to thyself images of men, and didst commit whoredom with them,

18 And tookest thy broidered garments, and coveredst them: and thou hast set mine oil and mine incense before them.

EZEKIEL

19 My meat also which I gave thee, fine flour, and oil, and honey, wherewith I fed thee, thou hast even set it before them for a sweet savour: and thus it was, saith the Lord GOD.

20 Moreover thou hast taken thy sons and thy daughters, whom thou hast borne unto me, and these hast thou sacrificed unto them to be devoured. Is this of thy whoredoms a small matter,

21 That thou hast slain my children, and delivered them to cause them to pass through the fire for them?

22 And in all thine abominations and thy whoredoms thou hast not remembered the days of thy youth, when thou wast naked and bare, and wast polluted in thy blood.

23 And it came to pass after all thy wickedness, (woe, woe unto thee! saith the Lord GOD;)

24 That thou hast also built unto thee an eminent place, and hast made thee an high place in every street.

EZEKIEL

25 Thou hast built thy high place at every head of the way, and hast made thy beauty to be abhorred, and hast opened thy feet to every one that passed by, and multiplied thy whoredoms.

26 Thou hast also committed fornication with the Egyptians thy neighbours, great of flesh; and hast increased thy whoredoms, to provoke me to anger.

27 Behold, therefore I have stretched out my hand over thee, and have diminished thine ordinary food, and delivered thee unto the will of them that hate thee, the daughters of the Philistines, which are ashamed of thy lewd way.

28 Thou hast played the whore also with the Assyrians, because thou wast unsatiable; yea, thou hast played the harlot with them, and yet couldest not be satisfied.

29 Thou hast moreover multiplied thy fornication in the land of Canaan unto Chaldea; and yet thou wast not satisfied herewith.

30 How weak is thine heart, saith the Lord GOD, seeing thou doest all these things, the work of an imperious whorish woman;

31 In that thou buildest thine eminent place in the head of every way, and makest thine high place in every street; and hast not been as an harlot, in that thou scornest hire;

32 But as a wife that committeth adultery, which taketh strangers instead of her husband!

33 They give gifts to all whores: but thou givest thy gifts to all thy lovers, and hirest them, that they may come unto thee on every side for thy whoredom.

34 And the contrary is in thee from other women in thy whoredoms, whereas none followeth thee to commit whoredoms: and in that thou givest a reward, and no reward is given unto thee, therefore thou art contrary.

35 Wherefore, O harlot, hear the word of the LORD:

EZEKIEL

36 Thus saith the Lord GOD; Because thy filthiness was poured out, and thy nakedness discovered through thy whoredoms with thy lovers, and with all the idols of thy abominations, and by the blood of thy children, which thou didst give unto them;

37 Behold, therefore I will gather all thy lovers, with whom thou hast taken pleasure, and all them that thou hast loved, with all them that thou hast hated; I will even gather them round about against thee, and will discover thy nakedness unto them, that they may see all thy nakedness.

38 And I will judge thee, as women that break wedlock and shed blood are judged; and I will give thee blood in fury and jealousy.

39 And I will also give thee into their hand, and they shall throw down thine eminent place, and shall break down thy high places: they shall strip thee also of thy clothes, and shall take thy fair jewels, and leave thee naked and bare.

40 They shall also bring up a company against thee, and they shall stone thee with stones, and thrust thee through with their swords.

41 And they shall burn thine houses with fire, and execute judgments upon thee in the sight of many women: and I will cause thee to cease from playing the harlot, and thou also shalt give no hire any more.

42 So will I make my fury toward thee to rest, and my jealousy shall depart from thee, and I will be quiet, and will be no more angry.

43 Because thou hast not remembered the days of thy youth, but hast fretted me in all these things; behold, therefore I also will recompense thy way upon thine head, saith the Lord GOD: and thou shalt not commit this lewdness above all thine abominations.

44 Behold, every one that useth proverbs shall use this proverb against thee, saying, As is the mother, so is her daughter.

EZEKIEL

45 Thou art thy mother's daughter, that loatheth her husband and her children; and thou art the sister of thy sisters, which loathed their husbands and their children: your mother was an Hittite, and your father an Amorite.

46 And thine elder sister is Samaria, she and her daughters that dwell at thy left hand: and thy younger sister, that dwelleth at thy right hand, is Sodom and her daughters.

47 Yet hast thou not walked after their ways, nor done after their abominations: but, as if that were a very little thing, thou wast corrupted more than they in all thy ways.

48 As I live, saith the Lord GOD, Sodom thy sister hath not done, she nor her daughters, as thou hast done, thou and thy daughters.

49 Behold, this was the iniquity of thy sister Sodom, pride, fulness of bread, and abundance of idleness was in her and in her daughters, neither did she strengthen the hand of the poor and needy.

EZEKIEL

50 And they were haughty, and committed abomination before me: therefore I took them away as I saw good.

51 Neither hath Samaria committed half of thy sins; but thou hast multiplied thine abominations more than they, and hast justified thy sisters in all thine abominations which thou hast done.

52 Thou also, which hast judged thy sisters, bear thine own shame for thy sins that thou hast committed more abominable than they: they are more righteous than thou: yea, be thou confounded also, and bear thy shame, in that thou hast justified thy sisters.

53 When I shall bring again their captivity, the captivity of Sodom and her daughters, and the captivity of Samaria and her daughters, then will I bring again the captivity of thy captives in the midst of them:

54 That thou mayest bear thine own shame, and mayest be confounded in all that thou hast done, in that thou art a comfort unto them.

5-5 When thy sisters, Sodom and her daughters, shall return to their former estate, and Samaria and her daughters shall return to their former estate, then thou and thy daughters shall return to your former estate.

5-6 For thy sister Sodom was not mentioned by thy mouth in the day of thy pride,

5-7 Before thy wickedness was discovered, as at the time of thy reproach of the daughters of Syria, and all that are round about her, the daughters of the Philistines, which despise thee round about.

5-8 Thou hast borne thy lewdness and thine abominations, saith the LORD.

5-9 For thus saith the Lord GOD; I will even deal with thee as thou hast done, which hast despised the oath in breaking the covenant.

6-0 Nevertheless I will remember my covenant with thee in the days of thy youth, and I will establish unto thee an everlasting covenant.

EZEKIEL

61 Then thou shalt remember thy ways, and be ashamed, when thou shalt receive thy sisters, thine elder and thy younger: and I will give them unto thee for daughters, but not by thy covenant.

62 And I will establish my covenant with thee; and thou shalt know that I am the LORD:

63 That thou mayest remember, and be confounded, and never open thy mouth any more because of thy shame, when I am pacified toward thee for all that thou hast done, saith the Lord GOD.

CHAPTER 17

1 And the word of the LORD came unto me, saying,

2 Son of man, put forth a riddle, and speak a parable unto the house of Israel;

3 And say, Thus saith the Lord GOD; A great eagle with great wings, longwinged, full of feathers, which had divers colours, came unto Lebanon, and took the highest branch of the cedar:

EZEKIEL

4 He cropped off the top of his young twigs, and carried it into a land of traffick; he set it in a city of merchants.

5 He took also of the seed of the land, and planted it in a fruitful field; he placed it by great waters, and set it as a willow tree.

6 And it grew, and became a spreading vine of low stature, whose branches turned toward him, and the roots thereof were under him: so it became a vine, and brought forth branches, and shot forth sprigs.

7 There was also another great eagle with great wings and many feathers: and, behold, this vine did bend her roots toward him, and shot forth her branches toward him, that he might water it by the furrows of her plantation.

8 It was planted in a good soil by great waters, that it might bring forth branches, and that it might bear fruit, that it might be a goodly vine.

EZEKIEL

9 Say thou, Thus saith the Lord GOD; Shall it prosper? shall he not pull up the roots thereof, and cut off the fruit thereof, that it wither? it shall wither in all the leaves of her spring, even without great power or many people to pluck it up by the roots thereof.

10 Yea, behold, being planted, shall it prosper? shall it not utterly wither, when the east wind toucheth it? it shall wither in the furrows where it grew.

11 Moreover the word of the LORD came unto me, saying,

12 Say now to the rebellious house, Know ye not what these things mean? tell them, Behold, the king of Babylon is come to Jerusalem, and hath taken the king thereof, and the princes thereof, and led them with him to Babylon;

13 And hath taken of the king's seed, and made a covenant with him, and hath taken an oath of him: he hath also taken the mighty of the land:

EZEKIEL

14 That the kingdom might be base, that it might not lift itself up, but that by keeping of his covenant it might stand.

15 But he rebelled against him in sending his ambassadors into Egypt, that they might give him horses and much people. Shall he prosper? shall he escape that doeth such things? or shall he break the covenant, and be delivered?

16 As I live, saith the Lord GOD, surely in the place where the king dwelleth that made him king, whose oath he despised, and whose covenant he brake, even with him in the midst of Babylon he shall die.

17 Neither shall Pharaoh with his mighty army and great company make for him in the war, by casting up mounts, and building forts, to cut off many persons:

18 Seeing he despised the oath by breaking the covenant, when, lo, he had given his hand, and hath done all these things, he shall not escape.

EZEKIEL

19 Therefore thus saith the Lord GOD; As I live, surely mine oath that he hath despised, and my covenant that he hath broken, even it will I recompense upon his own head.

20 And I will spread my net upon him, and he shall be taken in my snare, and I will bring him to Babylon, and will plead with him there for his trespass that he hath trespassed against me.

21 And all his fugitives with all his bands shall fall by the sword, and they that remain shall be scattered toward all winds: and ye shall know that I the LORD have spoken it.

22 Thus saith the Lord GOD; I will also take of the highest branch of the high cedar, and will set it; I will crop off from the top of his young twigs a tender one, and will plant it upon an high mountain and eminent:

23 In the mountain of the height of Israel will I plant it: and it shall bring forth boughs, and bear fruit, and be a goodly cedar: and under it shall dwell all fowl of every wing; in the shadow of the branches thereof shall they dwell.

EZEKIEL

24 And all the trees of the field shall know that I the
LORD have brought down the high tree, have exalted
the low tree, have dried up the green tree, and have
made the dry tree to flourish: I the LORD have
spoken and have done it.

CHAPTER 18

1 The word of the LORD came unto me again, saying,
2 What mean ye, that ye use this proverb concerning
the land of Israel, saying, The fathers have eaten sour
grapes, and the children's teeth are set on edge?
3 As I live, saith the Lord GOD, ye shall not have
occasion any more to use this proverb in Israel.
4 Behold, all souls are mine; as the soul of the father,
so also the soul of the son is mine: the soul that
sinneth, it shall die.
5 But if a man be just, and do that which is lawful
and right,

6 And hath not eaten upon the mountains, neither hath lifted up his eyes to the idols of the house of Israel, neither hath defiled his neighbour's wife, neither hath come near to a menstruous woman;

7 And hath not oppressed any, but hath restored to the debtor his pledge, hath spoiled none by violence, hath given his bread to the hungry, and hath covered the naked with a garment;

8 He that hath not given forth upon usury, neither hath taken any increase, that hath withdrawn his hand from iniquity, hath executed true judgment between man and man,

9 Hath walked in my statutes, and hath kept my judgments, to deal truly; he is just, he shall surely live, saith the Lord GOD.

10 If he beget a son that is a robber, a shedder of blood, and that doeth the like to any one of these things,

11 And that doeth not any of those duties, but even hath eaten upon the mountains, and defiled his neighbour's wife,

EZEKIEL

12 Hath oppressed the poor and needy, hath spoiled
by violence, hath not restored the pledge, and hath
lifted up his eyes to the idols, hath committed
abomination,

13 Hath given forth upon usury, and hath taken
increase: shall he then live? he shall not live: he hath
done all these abominations; he shall surely die; his
blood shall be upon him.

14 Now, lo, if he beget a son, that seeth all his
father's sins which he hath done, and considereth, and
doeth not such like,

15 That hath not eaten upon the mountains, neither
hath lifted up his eyes to the idols of the house of
Israel, hath not defiled his neighbour's wife,

16 Neither hath oppressed any, hath not withholden
the pledge, neither hath spoiled by violence, but hath
given his bread to the hungry, and hath covered the
naked with a garment,

EZEKIEL

17 That hath taken off his hand from the poor, that hath not received usury nor increase, hath executed my judgments, hath walked in my statutes; he shall not die for the iniquity of his father, he shall surely live.

18 As for his father, because he cruelly oppressed, spoiled his brother by violence, and did that which is not good among his people, lo, even he shall die in his iniquity.

19 Yet say ye, Why? doth not the son bear the iniquity of the father? When the son hath done that which is lawful and right, and hath kept all my statutes, and hath done them, he shall surely live.

20 The soul that sinneth, it shall die. The son shall not bear the iniquity of the father, neither shall the father bear the iniquity of the son: the righteousness of the righteous shall be upon him, and the wickedness of the wicked shall be upon him.

21 But if the wicked will turn from all his sins that he hath committed, and keep all my statutes, and do that which is lawful and right, he shall surely live, he shall not die.

EZEKIEL

22- All his transgressions that he hath committed, they shall not be mentioned unto him: in his righteousness that he hath done he shall live.

23- Have I any pleasure at all that the wicked should die? saith the Lord GOD: and not that he should return from his ways, and live?

24- But when the righteous turneth away from his righteousness, and committeth iniquity, and doeth according to all the abominations that the wicked man doeth, shall he live? All his righteousness that he hath done shall not be mentioned: in his trespass that he hath trespassed, and in his sin that he hath sinned, in them shall he die.

25- Yet ye say, The way of the Lord is not equal. Hear now, O house of Israel; Is not my way equal? are not your ways unequal?

26- When a righteous man turneth away from his righteousness, and committeth iniquity, and dieth in them; for his iniquity that he hath done shall he die.

EZEKIEL

27 Again, when the wicked man turneth away from his wickedness that he hath committed, and doeth that which is lawful and right, he shall save his soul alive.

28 Because he considereth, and turneth away from all his transgressions that he hath committed, he shall surely live, he shall not die.

29 Yet saith the house of Israel, The way of the Lord is not equal. O house of Israel, are not my ways equal? are not your ways unequal?

30 Therefore I will judge you, O house of Israel, every one according to his ways, saith the Lord GOD. Repent, and turn yourselves from all your transgressions; so iniquity shall not be your ruin.

31 Cast away from you all your transgressions, whereby ye have transgressed; and make you a new heart and a new spirit: for why will ye die, O house of Israel?

32 For I have no pleasure in the death of him that dieth, saith the Lord GOD: wherefore turn yourselves, and live ye.

CHAPTER 19

1 Moreover take thou up a lamentation for the princes of Israel,

2 And say, What is thy mother? A lioness: she lay down among lions, she nourished her whelps among young lions.

3 And she brought up one of her whelps: it became a young lion, and it learned to catch the prey; it devoured men.

4 The nations also heard of him; he was taken in their pit, and they brought him with chains unto the land of Egypt.

5 Now when she saw that she had waited, and her hope was lost, then she took another of her whelps, and made him a young lion.

6 And he went up and down among the lions, he became a young lion, and learned to catch the prey, and devoured men.

7 And he knew their desolate palaces, and he laid waste their cities; and the land was desolate, and the fulness thereof, by the noise of his roaring.

EZEKIEL

8 Then the nations set against him on every side from the provinces, and spread their net over him: he was taken in their pit.

9 And they put him in ward in chains, and brought him to the king of Babylon: they brought him into holds, that his voice should no more be heard upon the mountains of Israel.

10 Thy mother is like a vine in thy blood, planted by the waters: she was fruitful and full of branches by reason of many waters.

11 And she had strong rods for the sceptres of them that bare rule, and her stature was exalted among the thick branches, and she appeared in her height with the multitude of her branches.

12 But she was plucked up in fury, she was cast down to the ground, and the east wind dried up her fruit: her strong rods were broken and withered; the fire consumed them.

13 And now she is planted in the wilderness, in a dry and thirsty ground.

14 And fire is gone out of a rod of her branches, which hath devoured her fruit, so that she hath no strong rod to be a sceptre to rule. This is a lamentation, and shall be for a lamentation.

CHAPTER 20

1 And it came to pass in the seventh year, in the fifth month, the tenth day of the month, that certain of the elders of Israel came to enquire of the LORD, and sat before me.

2 Then came the word of the LORD unto me, saying,

3 Son of man, speak unto the elders of Israel, and say unto them, Thus saith the Lord GOD; Are ye come to enquire of me? As I live, saith the Lord GOD, I will not be enquired of by you.

4 Wilt thou judge them, son of man, wilt thou judge them? cause them to know the abominations of their fathers:

EZEKIEL

5 And say unto them, Thus saith the Lord GOD; In the day when I chose Israel, and lifted up mine hand unto the seed of the house of Jacob, and made myself known unto them in the land of Egypt, when I lifted up mine hand unto them, saying, I am the LORD your God.

6 In the day that I lifted up mine hand unto them, to bring them forth of the land of Egypt into a land that I had espied for them, flowing with milk and honey, which is the glory of all lands:

7 Then said I unto them, Cast ye away every man the abominations of his eyes, and defile not yourselves with the idols of Egypt: I am the LORD your God.

EZEKIEL

8 But they rebelled against me, and would not hearken unto me: they did not every man cast away the abominations of their eyes, neither did they forsake the idols of Egypt: then I said, I will pour out my fury upon them, to accomplish my anger against them in the midst of the land of Egypt.

9 But I wrought for my name's sake, that it should not be polluted before the heathen, among whom they were, in whose sight I made myself known unto them, in bringing them forth out of the land of Egypt.

10 Wherefore I caused them to go forth out of the land of Egypt, and brought them into the wilderness.

11 And I gave them my statutes, and shewed them my judgments, which if a man do, he shall even live in them.

12 Moreover also I gave them my sabbaths, to be a sign between me and them, that they might know that I am the LORD that sanctify them.

EZEKIEL

13 But the house of Israel rebelled against me in the wilderness: they walked not in my statutes, and they despised my judgments, which if a man do, he shall even live in them: and my sabbaths they greatly polluted: then I said, I would pour out my fury upon them in the wilderness, to consume them.

14 But I wrought for my name's sake, that it should not be polluted before the heathen, in whose sight I brought them out.

15 Yet also I lifted up my hand unto them in the wilderness, that I would not bring them into the land which I had given them, flowing with milk and honey, which is the glory of all lands;

16 Because they despised my judgments, and walked not in my statutes, but polluted my sabbaths: for their heart went after their idols.

17 Nevertheless mine eye spared them from destroying them, neither did I make an end of them in the wilderness.

EZEKIEL

18 But I said unto their children in the wilderness, Walk ye not in the statutes of your fathers, neither observe their judgments, nor defile yourselves with their idols:

19 I am the LORD your God; walk in my statutes, and keep my judgments, and do them;

20 And hallow my sabbaths; and they shall be a sign between me and you, that ye may know that I am the LORD your God.

21 Notwithstanding the children rebelled against me: they walked not in my statutes, neither kept my judgments to do them, which if a man do, he shall even live in them; they polluted my sabbaths: then I said, I would pour out my fury upon them, to accomplish my anger against them in the wilderness.

22 Nevertheless I withdrew mine hand, and wrought for my name's sake, that it should not be polluted in the sight of the heathen, in whose sight I brought them forth.

23 I lifted up mine hand unto them also in the wilderness, that I would scatter them among the heathen, and disperse them through the countries:

24 Because they had not executed my judgments, but had despised my statutes, and had polluted my sabbaths, and their eyes were after their fathers' idols.

25 Wherefore I gave them also statutes that were not good, and judgments whereby they should not live;

26 And I polluted them in their own gifts, in that they caused to pass through the fire all that openeth the womb, that I might make them desolate, to the end that they might know that I am the LORD.

27 Therefore, son of man, speak unto the house of Israel, and say unto them, Thus saith the Lord GOD; Yet in this your fathers have blasphemed me, in that they have committed a trespass against me.

EZEKIEL

28 For when I had brought them into the land, for the which I lifted up mine hand to give it to them, then they saw every high hill, and all the thick trees, and they offered there their sacrifices, and there they presented the provocation of their offering: there also they made their sweet savour, and poured out there their drink offerings.

29 Then I said unto them, What is the high place whereunto ye go? And the name thereof is called Bamah unto this day.

30 Wherefore say unto the house of Israel, Thus saith the Lord GOD; Are ye polluted after the manner of your fathers? and commit ye whoredom after their abominations?

31 For when ye offer your gifts, when ye make your sons to pass through the fire, ye pollute yourselves with all your idols, even unto this day: and shall I be enquired of by you, O house of Israel? As I live, saith the Lord GOD, I will not be enquired of by you.

EZEKIEL

3-2 And that which cometh into your mind shall not be at all, that ye say, We will be as the heathen, as the families of the countries, to serve wood and stone.

3-3 As I live, saith the Lord GOD, surely with a mighty hand, and with a stretched out arm, and with fury poured out, will I rule over you:

3-4 And I will bring you out from the people, and will gather you out of the countries wherein ye are scattered, with a mighty hand, and with a stretched out arm, and with fury poured out.

3-5 And I will bring you into the wilderness of the people, and there will I plead with you face to face.

3-6 Like as I pleaded with your fathers in the wilderness of the land of Egypt, so will I plead with you, saith the Lord GOD.

3-7 And I will cause you to pass under the rod, and I will bring you into the bond of the covenant:

EZEKIEL

38 And I will purge out from among you the rebels, and them that transgress against me: I will bring them forth out of the country where they sojourn, and they shall not enter into the land of Israel: and ye shall know that I am the LORD.

39 As for you, O house of Israel, thus saith the Lord GOD; Go ye, serve ye every one his idols, and hereafter also, if ye will not hearken unto me: but pollute ye my holy name no more with your gifts, and with your idols.

40 For in mine holy mountain, in the mountain of the height of Israel, saith the Lord GOD, there shall all the house of Israel, all of them in the land, serve me: there will I accept them, and there will I require your offerings, and the firstfruits of your oblations, with all your holy things.

EZEKIEL

41 I will accept you with your sweet savour, when I bring you out from the people, and gather you out of the countries wherein ye have been scattered; and I will be sanctified in you before the heathen.

42 And ye shall know that I am the LORD, when I shall bring you into the land of Israel, into the country for the which I lifted up mine hand to give it to your fathers.

43 And there shall ye remember your ways, and all your doings, wherein ye have been defiled; and ye shall lothe yourselves in your own sight for all your evils that ye have committed.

44 And ye shall know that I am the LORD, when I have wrought with you for my name's sake, not according to your wicked ways, nor according to your corrupt doings, O ye house of Israel, saith the Lord GOD.

45 Moreover the word of the LORD came unto me, saying,

EZEKIEL

46 Son of man, set thy face toward the south, and
drop thy word toward the south, and prophesy
against the forest of the south field;

47 And say to the forest of the south, Hear the word
of the LORD; Thus saith the Lord GOD; Behold, I
will kindle a fire in thee, and it shall devour every
green tree in thee, and every dry tree: the flaming
flame shall not be quenched, and all faces from the
south to the north shall be burned therein.

48 And all flesh shall see that I the LORD have
kindled it: it shall not be quenched.

49 Then said I, Ah Lord GOD! they say of me, Doth
he not speak parables?

CHAPTER 21

1 And the word of the LORD came unto me, saying,

2 Son of man, set thy face toward Jerusalem, and
drop thy word toward the holy places, and prophesy
against the land of Israel,

EZEKIEL

3 And say to the land of Israel, Thus saith the LORD; Behold, I am against thee, and will draw forth my sword out of his sheath, and will cut off from thee the righteous and the wicked.

4 Seeing then that I will cut off from thee the righteous and the wicked, therefore shall my sword go forth out of his sheath against all flesh from the south to the north:

5 That all flesh may know that I the LORD have drawn forth my sword out of his sheath: it shall not return any more.

6 Sigh therefore, thou son of man, with the breaking of thy loins; and with bitterness sigh before their eyes.

7 And it shall be, when they say unto thee, Wherefore sighest thou? that thou shalt answer, For the tidings; because it cometh: and every heart shall melt, and all hands shall be feeble, and every spirit shall faint, and all knees shall be weak as water: behold, it cometh, and shall be brought to pass, saith the Lord GOD.

EZEKIEL

8 Again the word of the LORD came unto me, saying,

9 Son of man, prophesy, and say, Thus saith the LORD; Say, A sword, a sword is sharpened, and also furbished:

10 It is sharpened to make a sore slaughter; it is furbished that it may glitter: should we then make mirth? it contemneth the rod of my son, as every tree.

11 And he hath given it to be furbished, that it may be handled: this sword is sharpened, and it is furbished, to give it into the hand of the slayer.

12 Cry and howl, son of man: for it shall be upon my people, it shall be upon all the princes of Israel: terrors by reason of the sword shall be upon my people: smite therefore upon thy thigh.

13 Because it is a trial, and what if the sword contemn even the rod? it shall be no more, saith the Lord GOD.

EZEKIEL

14 Thou therefore, son of man, prophesy, and smite thine hands together, and let the sword be doubled the third time, the sword of the slain: it is the sword of the great men that are slain, which entereth into their privy chambers.

15 I have set the point of the sword against all their gates, that their heart may faint, and their ruins be multiplied: ah! it is made bright, it is wrapped up for the slaughter.

16 Go thee one way or other, either on the right hand, or on the left, whithersoever thy face is set.

17 I will also smite mine hands together, and I will cause my fury to rest: I the LORD have said it.

18 The word of the LORD came unto me again, saying,

19 Also, thou son of man, appoint thee two ways, that the sword of the king of Babylon may come: both twain shall come forth out of one land: and choose thou a place, choose it at the head of the way to the city.

20 Appoint a way, that the sword may come to Rabbath of the Ammonites, and to Judah in Jerusalem the defenced.

21 For the king of Babylon stood at the parting of the way, at the head of the two ways, to use divination: he made his arrows bright, he consulted with images, he looked in the liver.

22 At his right hand was the divination for Jerusalem, to appoint captains, to open the mouth in the slaughter, to lift up the voice with shouting, to appoint battering rams against the gates, to cast a mount, and to build a fort.

23 And it shall be unto them as a false divination in their sight, to them that have sworn oaths: but he will call to remembrance the iniquity, that they may be taken.

24 Therefore thus saith the Lord GOD; Because ye have made your iniquity to be remembered, in that your transgressions are discovered, so that in all your doings your sins do appear; because, I say, that ye are come to remembrance, ye shall be taken with the hand.

25 And thou, profane wicked prince of Israel, whose day is come, when iniquity shall have an end,

26 Thus saith the Lord GOD; Remove the diadem, and take off the crown: this shall not be the same: exalt him that is low, and abase him that is high.

27 I will overturn, overturn, overturn, it: and it shall be no more, until he come whose right it is; and I will give it him.

EZEKIEL

2:8 - And thou, son of man, prophesy and say, Thus saith the Lord GOD concerning the Ammonites, and concerning their reproach; even say thou, The sword, the sword is drawn: for the slaughter it is furbished, to consume because of the glittering:

2:9 Whiles they see vanity unto thee, whiles they divine a lie unto thee, to bring thee upon the necks of them that are slain, of the wicked, whose day is come, when their iniquity shall have an end.

3:0 Shall I cause it to return into his sheath? I will judge thee in the place where thou wast created, in the land of thy nativity.

3:1 And I will pour out mine indignation upon thee, I will blow against thee in the fire of my wrath, and deliver thee into the hand of brutish men, and skilful to destroy.

3:2 Thou shalt be for fuel to the fire; thy blood shall be in the midst of the land; thou shalt be no more remembered: for I the LORD have spoken it.

EZEKIEL

CHAPTER 22

1 Moreover the word of the LORD came unto me, saying,

2 Now, thou son of man, wilt thou judge, wilt thou judge the bloody city? yea, thou shalt shew her all her abominations.

3 Then say thou, Thus saith the Lord GOD, The city sheddeth blood in the midst of it, that her time may come, and maketh idols against herself to defile herself.

4 Thou art become guilty in thy blood that thou hast shed; and hast defiled thyself in thine idols which thou hast made; and thou hast caused thy days to draw near, and art come even unto thy years: therefore have I made thee a reproach unto the heathen, and a mocking to all countries.

5 Those that be near, and those that be far from thee, shall mock thee, which art infamous and much vexed.

6 Behold, the princes of Israel, every one were in thee to their power to shed blood.

EZEKIEL

7 In thee have they set light by father and mother: in the midst of thee have they dealt by oppression with the stranger: in thee have they vexed the fatherless and the widow.

8 Thou hast despised mine holy things, and hast profaned my sabbaths.

9 In thee are men that carry tales to shed blood: and in thee they eat upon the mountains: in the midst of thee they commit lewdness.

10 In thee have they discovered their fathers' nakedness: in thee have they humbled her that was set apart for pollution.

11 And one hath committed abomination with his neighbour's wife; and another hath lewdly defiled his daughter in law; and another in thee hath humbled his sister, his father's daughter.

12 In thee have they taken gifts to shed blood; thou hast taken usury and increase, and thou hast greedily gained of thy neighbours by extortion, and hast forgotten me, saith the Lord GOD.

EZEKIEL

13 Behold, therefore I have smitten mine hand at thy dishonest gain which thou hast made, and at thy blood which hath been in the midst of thee.

14 Can thine heart endure, or can thine hands be strong, in the days that I shall deal with thee? I the LORD have spoken it, and will do it.

15 And I will scatter thee among the heathen, and disperse thee in the countries, and will consume thy filthiness out of thee.

16 And thou shalt take thine inheritance in thyself in the sight of the heathen, and thou shalt know that I am the LORD.

17 And the word of the LORD came unto me, saying,

18 Son of man, the house of Israel is to me become dross: all they are brass, and tin, and iron, and lead, in the midst of the furnace; they are even the dross of silver.

EZEKIEL

19 Therefore thus saith the Lord GOD; Because ye are all become dross, behold, therefore I will gather you into the midst of Jerusalem.

20 As they gather silver, and brass, and iron, and lead, and tin, into the midst of the furnace, to blow the fire upon it, to melt it; so will I gather you in mine anger and in my fury, and I will leave you there, and melt you.

21 Yea, I will gather you, and blow upon you in the fire of my wrath, and ye shall be melted in the midst thereof.

22 As silver is melted in the midst of the furnace, so shall ye be melted in the midst thereof; and ye shall know that I the LORD have poured out my fury upon you.

23 And the word of the LORD came unto me, saying,

24 Son of man, say unto her, Thou art the land that is not cleansed, nor rained upon in the day of indignation.

EZEKIEL

2:5 There is a conspiracy of her prophets in the midst thereof, like a roaring lion ravening the prey; they have devoured souls; they have taken the treasure and precious things; they have made her many widows in the midst thereof.

2:6 Her priests have violated my law, and have profaned mine holy things: they have put no difference between the holy and profane, neither have they shewed difference between the unclean and the clean, and have hid their eyes from my sabbaths, and I am profaned among them.

2:7 Her princes in the midst thereof are like wolves ravening the prey, to shed blood, and to destroy souls, to get dishonest gain.

2:8 And her prophets have daubed them with untempered morter, seeing vanity, and divining lies unto them, saying, Thus saith the Lord GOD, when the LORD hath not spoken.

EZEKIEL

29 The people of the land have used oppression, and exercised robbery, and have vexed the poor and needy: yea, they have oppressed the stranger wrongfully.

30 And I sought for a man among them, that should make up the hedge, and stand in the gap before me for the land, that I should not destroy it: but I found none.

31 Therefore have I poured out mine indignation upon them; I have consumed them with the fire of my wrath: their own way have I recompensed upon their heads, saith the Lord GOD.

CHAPTER 23

1 The word of the LORD came again unto me, saying,

2 Son of man, there were two women, the daughters of one mother:

3 And they committed whoredoms in Egypt: they
committed whoredoms in their youth: there were their
breasts pressed, and there they bruised the teats of
their virginity.

4 And the names of them were; Aholah the elder, and
Aholibah her sister: and they were mine, and they
bare sons and daughters. Thus were their names;
Samaria is Aholah, and Jerusalem Aholibah.

5 And Aholah played the harlot when she was mine;
and she doted on her lovers, on the Assyrians her
neighbours,

6 Which were clothed with blue, captains and rulers, all
of them desirable young men, horsemen riding upon
horses.

7 Thus she committed her whoredoms with them, with
all them that were the chosen men of Assyria, and
with all on whom she doted: with all their idols she
defiled herself.

8 Neither left she her whoredoms brought from Egypt: for in her youth they lay with her, and they bruised the breasts of her virginity, and poured their whoredom upon her.

9 Wherefore I have delivered her into the hand of her lovers, into the hand of the Assyrians, upon whom she doted.

10 These discovered her nakedness: they took her sons and her daughters, and slew her with the sword: and she became famous among women; for they had executed judgment upon her.

11 And when her sister Aholibah saw this, she was more corrupt in her inordinate love than she, and in her whoredoms more than her sister in her whoredoms.

12 She doted upon the Assyrians her neighbours, captains and rulers clothed most gorgeously, horsemen riding upon horses, all of them desirable young men.

13 Then I saw that she was defiled, that they took both one way,

14 And that she increased her whoredoms: for when she saw men pourtrayed upon the wall, the images of the Chaldeans pourtrayed with vermilion,

15 Girded with girdles upon their loins, exceeding in dyed attire upon their heads, all of them princes to look to, after the manner of the Babylonians of Chaldea, the land of their nativity:

16 And as soon as she saw them with her eyes, she doted upon them, and sent messengers unto them into Chaldea.

17 And the Babylonians came to her into the bed of love, and they defiled her with their whoredom, and she was polluted with them, and her mind was alienated from them.

18 So she discovered her whoredoms, and discovered her nakedness: then my mind was alienated from her, like as my mind was alienated from her sister.

19 Yet she multiplied her whoredoms, in calling to remembrance the days of her youth, wherein she had played the harlot in the land of Egypt.

20 For she doted upon their paramours, whose flesh is as the flesh of asses, and whose issue is like the issue of horses.

21 Thus thou calledst to remembrance the lewdness of thy youth, in bruising thy teats by the Egyptians for the paps of thy youth.

22 Therefore, O Aholibah, thus saith the Lord GOD; Behold, I will raise up thy lovers against thee, from whom thy mind is alienated, and I will bring them against thee on every side;

23 The Babylonians, and all the Chaldeans, Pekod, and Shoa, and Koa, and all the Assyrians with them: all of them desirable young men, captains and rulers, great lords and renowned, all of them riding upon horses.

EZEKIEL

24 And they shall come against thee with chariots, wagons, and wheels, and with an assembly of people, which shall set against thee buckler and shield and helmet round about: and I will set judgment before them, and they shall judge thee according to their judgments.

25 And I will set my jealousy against thee, and they shall deal furiously with thee: they shall take away thy nose and thine ears; and thy remnant shall fall by the sword: they shall take thy sons and thy daughters; and thy residue shall be devoured by the fire.

26 They shall also strip thee out of thy clothes, and take away thy fair jewels.

27 Thus will I make thy lewdness to cease from thee, and thy whoredom brought from the land of Egypt: so that thou shalt not lift up thine eyes unto them, nor remember Egypt any more.

EZEKIEL

28 For thus saith the Lord GOD; Behold, I will deliver thee into the hand of them whom thou hatest, into the hand of them from whom thy mind is alienated:

29 And they shall deal with thee hatefully, and shall take away all thy labour, and shall leave thee naked and bare: and the nakedness of thy whoredoms shall be discovered, both thy lewdness and thy whoredoms.

30 I will do these things unto thee, because thou hast gone a whoring after the heathen, and because thou art polluted with their idols.

31 Thou hast walked in the way of thy sister; therefore will I give her cup into thine hand.

32 Thus saith the Lord GOD; Thou shalt drink of thy sister's cup deep and large: thou shalt be laughed to scorn and had in derision; it containeth much.

33 Thou shalt be filled with drunkenness and sorrow, with the cup of astonishment and desolation, with the cup of thy sister Samaria.

EZEKIEL

23:4 Thou shalt even drink it and suck it out, and thou shalt break the sherds thereof, and pluck off thine own breasts: for I have spoken it, saith the Lord GOD.

23:5 Therefore thus saith the Lord GOD; Because thou hast forgotten me, and cast me behind thy back, therefore bear thou also thy lewdness and thy whoredoms.

23:6 The LORD said moreover unto me, Son of man, wilt thou judge Aholah and Aholibah? yea, declare unto them their abominations;

23:7 That they have committed adultery, and blood is in their hands, and with their idols have they committed adultery, and have also caused their sons, whom they bare unto me, to pass for them through the fire, to devour them.

23:8 Moreover this they have done unto me: they have defiled my sanctuary in the same day, and have profaned my sabbaths.

EZEKIEL

39 For when they had slain their children to their
idols, then they came the same day into my sanctuary
to profane it; and, lo, thus have they done in the midst
of mine house.

40 And furthermore, that ye have sent for men to
come from far, unto whom a messenger was sent; and,
lo, they came: for whom thou didst wash thyself,
paintedst thy eyes, and deckedst thyself with
ornaments,

41 And satest upon a stately bed, and a table
prepared before it, whereupon thou hast set mine
incense and mine oil.

42 And a voice of a multitude being at ease was with
her: and with the men of the common sort were
brought Sabeans from the wilderness, which put
bracelets upon their hands, and beautiful crowns upon
their heads.

43 Then said I unto her that was old in adulteries,
Will they now commit whoredoms with her, and she
with them?

44 Yet they went in unto her, as they go in unto a woman that playeth the harlot: so went they in unto Aholah and unto Aholibah, the lewd women.

45 And the righteous men, they shall judge them after the manner of adulteresses, and after the manner of women that shed blood; because they are adulteresses, and blood is in their hands.

46 For thus saith the Lord GOD; I will bring up a company upon them, and will give them to be removed and spoiled.

47 And the company shall stone them with stones, and dispatch them with their swords; they shall slay their sons and their daughters, and burn up their houses with fire.

48 Thus will I cause lewdness to cease out of the land, that all women may be taught not to do after your lewdness.

49 And they shall recompense your lewdness upon you, and ye shall bear the sins of your idols: and ye shall know that I am the Lord GOD.

CHAPTER 24

1 Again in the ninth year, in the tenth month, in the tenth day of the month, the word of the LORD came unto me, saying,

2 Son of man, write thee the name of the day, even of this same day: the king of Babylon set himself against Jerusalem this same day.

3 And utter a parable unto the rebellious house, and say unto them, Thus saith the Lord GOD; Set on a pot, set it on, and also pour water into it:

4 Gather the pieces thereof into it, even every good piece, the thigh, and the shoulder; fill it with the choice bones.

5 Take the choice of the flock, and burn also the bones under it, and make it boil well, and let them seethe the bones of it therein.

EZEKIEL

6 Wherefore thus saith the Lord GOD; Woe to the bloody city, to the pot whose scum is therein, and whose scum is not gone out of it! bring it out piece by piece; let no lot fall upon it.

7 For her blood is in the midst of her; she set it upon the top of a rock; she poured it not upon the ground, to cover it with dust;

8 That it might cause fury to come up to take vengeance; I have set her blood upon the top of a rock, that it should not be covered.

9 Therefore thus saith the Lord GOD; Woe to the bloody city! I will even make the pile for fire great.

10 Heap on wood, kindle the fire, consume the flesh, and spice it well, and let the bones be burned.

11 Then set it empty upon the coals thereof, that the brass of it may be hot, and may burn, and that the filthiness of it may be molten in it, that the scum of it may be consumed.

EZEKIEL

12 She hath wearied herself with lies, and her great scum went not forth out of her: her scum shall be in the fire.

13 In thy filthiness is lewdness: because I have purged thee, and thou wast not purged, thou shalt not be purged from thy filthiness any more, till I have caused my fury to rest upon thee.

14 I the LORD have spoken it: it shall come to pass, and I will do it; I will not go back, neither will I spare, neither will I repent; according to thy ways, and according to thy doings, shall they judge thee, saith the Lord GOD.

15 Also the word of the LORD came unto me, saying,

16 Son of man, behold, I take away from thee the desire of thine eyes with a stroke: yet neither shalt thou mourn nor weep, neither shall thy tears run down.

EZEKIEL

17 Forbear to cry, make no mourning for the dead, bind the tire of thine head upon thee, and put on thy shoes upon thy feet, and cover not thy lips, and eat not the bread of men.

18 So I spake unto the people in the morning: and at even my wife died; and I did in the morning as I was commanded.

19 And the people said unto me, Wilt thou not tell us what these things are to us, that thou doest so?

20 Then I answered them, The word of the LORD came unto me, saying,

21 Speak unto the house of Israel, Thus saith the Lord GOD; Behold, I will profane my sanctuary, the excellency of your strength, the desire of your eyes, and that which your soul pitieth; and your sons and your daughters whom ye have left shall fall by the sword.

22 And ye shall do as I have done: ye shall not cover your lips, nor eat the bread of men.

EZEKIEL

23 And your tires shall be upon your heads, and your shoes upon your feet: ye shall not mourn nor weep; but ye shall pine away for your iniquities, and mourn one toward another.

24 Thus Ezekiel is unto you a sign: according to all that he hath done shall ye do: and when this cometh, ye shall know that I am the Lord GOD.

25 Also, thou son of man, shall it not be in the day when I take from them their strength, the joy of their glory, the desire of their eyes, and that whereupon they set their minds, their sons and their daughters,

26 That he that escapeth in that day shall come unto thee, to cause thee to hear it with thine ears?

27 In that day shall thy mouth be opened to him which is escaped, and thou shalt speak, and be no more dumb: and thou shalt be a sign unto them; and they shall know that I am the LORD.

CHAPTER 25

1 The word of the LORD came again unto me, saying,

2 Son of man, set thy face against the Ammonites, and prophesy against them;

3 And say unto the Ammonites, Hear the word of the Lord GOD; Thus saith the Lord GOD; Because thou saidst, Aha, against my sanctuary, when it was profaned; and against the land of Israel, when it was desolate; and against the house of Judah, when they went into captivity;

4 Behold, therefore I will deliver thee to the men of the east for a possession, and they shall set their palaces in thee, and make their dwellings in thee: they shall eat thy fruit, and they shall drink thy milk.

5 And I will make Rabbah a stable for camels, and the Ammonites a couchingplace for flocks: and ye shall know that I am the LORD.

EZEKIEL

6 For thus saith the Lord GOD; Because thou hast clapped thine hands, and stamped with the feet, and rejoiced in heart with all thy despite against the land of Israel;

7 Behold, therefore I will stretch out mine hand upon thee, and will deliver thee for a spoil to the heathen; and I will cut thee off from the people, and I will cause thee to perish out of the countries: I will destroy thee; and thou shalt know that I am the LORD.

8 Thus saith the Lord GOD; Because that Moab and Seir do say, Behold, the house of Judah is like unto all the heathen;

9 Therefore, behold, I will open the side of Moab from the cities, from his cities which are on his frontiers, the glory of the country, Beth-jeshimoth, Baal-meon, and Kiriathaim,

10 Unto the men of the east with the Ammonites, and will give them in possession, that the Ammonites may not be remembered among the nations.

EZEKIEL

11 And I will execute judgments upon Moab; and they shall know that I am the LORD.

12 Thus saith the Lord GOD; Because that Edom hath dealt against the house of Judah by taking vengeance, and hath greatly offended, and revenged himself upon them;

13 Therefore thus saith the Lord GOD; I will also stretch out mine hand upon Edom, and will cut off man and beast from it; and I will make it desolate from Teman; and they of Dedan shall fall by the sword.

14 And I will lay my vengeance upon Edom by the hand of my people Israel: and they shall do in Edom according to mine anger and according to my fury; and they shall know my vengeance, saith the Lord GOD.

15 Thus saith the Lord GOD; Because the Philistines have dealt by revenge, and have taken vengeance with a despiteful heart, to destroy it for the old hatred;

EZEKIEL

16 Therefore thus saith the Lord GOD; Behold, I will stretch out mine hand upon the Philistines, and I will cut off the Cherethims, and destroy the remnant of the sea coast.

17 And I will execute great vengeance upon them with furious rebukes; and they shall know that I am the LORD, when I shall lay my vengeance upon them.

CHAPTER 26

1 And it came to pass in the eleventh year, in the first day of the month, that the word of the LORD came unto me, saying,

2 Son of man, because that Tyrus hath said against Jerusalem, Aha, she is broken that was the gates of the people: she is turned unto me: I shall be replenished, now she is laid waste:

3 Therefore thus saith the Lord GOD; Behold, I am against thee, O Tyrus, and will cause many nations to come up against thee, as the sea causeth his waves to come up.

EZEKIEL

4 And they shall destroy the walls of Tyrus, and break down her towers: I will also scrape her dust from her, and make her like the top of a rock.

5 It shall be a place for the spreading of nets in the midst of the sea: for I have spoken it, saith the Lord GOD: and it shall become a spoil to the nations.

6 And her daughters which are in the field shall be slain by the sword; and they shall know that I am the LORD.

7 For thus saith the Lord GOD; Behold, I will bring upon Tyrus Nebuchadrezzar king of Babylon, a king of kings, from the north, with horses, and with chariots, and with horsemen, and companies, and much people.

8 He shall slay with the sword thy daughters in the field: and he shall make a fort against thee, and cast a mount against thee, and lift up the buckler against thee.

EZEKIEL

9 And he shall set engines of war against thy walls, and with his axes he shall break down thy towers.

10 By reason of the abundance of his horses their dust shall cover thee: thy walls shall shake at the noise of the horsemen, and of the wheels, and of the chariots, when he shall enter into thy gates, as men enter into a city wherein is made a breach.

11 With the hoofs of his horses shall he tread down all thy streets: he shall slay thy people by the sword, and thy strong garrisons shall go down to the ground.

12 And they shall make a spoil of thy riches, and make a prey of thy merchandise: and they shall break down thy walls, and destroy thy pleasant houses: and they shall lay thy stones and thy timber and thy dust in the midst of the water.

13 And I will cause the noise of thy songs to cease; and the sound of thy harps shall be no more heard.

EZEKIEL

14 And I will make thee like the top of a rock: thou shalt be a place to spread nets upon; thou shalt be built no more: for I the LORD have spoken it, saith the Lord GOD.

15 Thus saith the Lord GOD to Tyrus; Shall not the isles shake at the sound of thy fall, when the wounded cry, when the slaughter is made in the midst of thee?

16 Then all the princes of the sea shall come down from their thrones, and lay away their robes, and put off their broidered garments: they shall clothe themselves with trembling; they shall sit upon the ground, and shall tremble at every moment, and be astonished at thee.

17 And they shall take up a lamentation for thee, and say to thee, How art thou destroyed, that wast inhabited of seafaring men, the renowned city, which wast strong in the sea, she and her inhabitants, which cause their terror to be on all that haunt it!

EZEKIEL

18 Now shall the isles tremble in the day of thy fall; yea, the isles that are in the sea shall be troubled at thy departure.

19 For thus saith the Lord GOD; When I shall make thee a desolate city, like the cities that are not inhabited; when I shall bring up the deep upon thee, and great waters shall cover thee;

20 When I shall bring thee down with them that descend into the pit, with the people of old time, and shall set thee in the low parts of the earth, in places desolate of old, with them that go down to the pit, that thou be not inhabited; and I shall set glory in the land of the living;

21 I will make thee a terror, and thou shalt be no more: though thou be sought for, yet shalt thou never be found again, saith the Lord GOD.

EZEKIEL

CHAPTER 27

1 The word of the LORD came again unto me, saying,

2 Now, thou son of man, take up a lamentation for Tyrus;

3 And say unto Tyrus, O thou that art situate at the entry of the sea, which art a merchant of the people for many isles, Thus saith the Lord GOD, O Tyrus, thou hast said, I am of perfect beauty.

4 Thy borders are in the midst of the seas, thy builders have perfected thy beauty.

5 They have made all thy ship boards of fir trees of Senir: they have taken cedars from Lebanon to make masts for thee.

6 Of the oaks of Bashan have they made thine oars; the company of the Ashurites have made thy benches of ivory, brought out of the isles of Chittim.

EZEKIEL

7 Fine linen with broidered work from Egypt was that which thou spreadest forth to be thy sail; blue and purple from the isles of Elishah was that which covered thee.

8 The inhabitants of Zidon and Arvad were thy mariners: thy wise men, O Tyrus, that were in thee, were thy pilots.

9 The ancients of Gebal and the wise men thereof were in thee thy calkers: all the ships of the sea with their mariners were in thee to occupy thy merchandise.

10 They of Persia and of Lud and of Phut were in thine army, thy men of war: they hanged the shield and helmet in thee; they set forth thy comeliness.

11 The men of Arvad with thine army were upon thy walls round about, and the Gammadims were in thy towers: they hanged their shields upon thy walls round about; they have made thy beauty perfect.

EZEKIEL

12 Tarshish was thy merchant by reason of the multitude of all kind of riches; with silver, iron, tin, and lead, they traded in thy fairs.

13 Javan, Tubal, and Meshech, they were thy merchants: they traded the persons of men and vessels of brass in thy market.

14 They of the house of Togarmah traded in thy fairs with horses and horsemen and mules.

15 The men of Dedan were thy merchants; many isles were the merchandise of thine hand: they brought thee for a present horns of ivory and ebony.

16 Syria was thy merchant by reason of the multitude of the wares of thy making: they occupied in thy fairs with emeralds, purple, and broidered work, and fine linen, and coral, and agate.

17 Judah, and the land of Israel, they were thy merchants: they traded in thy market wheat of Minnith, and Pannag, and honey, and oil, and balm.

EZEKIEL

18 Damascus was thy merchant in the multitude of the wares of thy making, for the multitude of all riches; in the wine of Helbon, and white wool.

19 Dan also and Javan going to and fro occupied in thy fairs: bright iron, cassia, and calamus, were in thy market.

20 Dedan was thy merchant in precious clothes for chariots.

21 Arabia, and all the princes of Kedar, they occupied with thee in lambs, and rams, and goats: in these were they thy merchants.

22 The merchants of Sheba and Raamah, they were thy merchants: they occupied in thy fairs with chief of all spices, and with all precious stones, and gold.

23 Haran, and Canneh, and Eden, the merchants of Sheba, Asshur, and Chilmad, were thy merchants.

EZEKIEL

24 These were thy merchants in all sorts of things, in blue clothes, and broidered work, and in chests of rich apparel, bound with cords, and made of cedar, among thy merchandise.

25 The ships of Tarshish did sing of thee in thy market: and thou wast replenished, and made very glorious in the midst of the seas.

26 Thy rowers have brought thee into great waters: the east wind hath broken thee in the midst of the seas.

27 Thy riches, and thy fairs, thy merchandise, thy mariners, and thy pilots, thy calkers, and the occupiers of thy merchandise, and all thy men of war, that are in thee, and in all thy company which is in the midst of thee, shall fall into the midst of the seas in the day of thy ruin.

28 The suburbs shall shake at the sound of the cry of thy pilots.

EZEKIEL

29 And all that handle the oar, the mariners, and all the pilots of the sea, shall come down from their ships, they shall stand upon the land;

30 And shall cause their voice to be heard against thee, and shall cry bitterly, and shall cast up dust upon their heads, they shall wallow themselves in the ashes:

31 And they shall make themselves utterly bald for thee, and gird them with sackcloth, and they shall weep for thee with bitterness of heart and bitter wailing.

32 And in their wailing they shall take up a lamentation for thee, and lament over thee, saying, What city is like Tyrus, like the destroyed in the midst of the sea?

33 When thy wares went forth out of the seas, thou filledst many people; thou didst enrich the kings of the earth with the multitude of thy riches and of thy merchandise.

EZEKIEL

34 In the time when thou shalt be broken by the seas in the depths of the waters thy merchandise and all thy company in the midst of thee shall fall.

35 All the inhabitants of the isles shall be astonished at thee, and their kings shall be sore afraid, they shall be troubled in their countenance.

36 The merchants among the people shall hiss at thee, thou shalt be a terror, and never shalt be any more.

CHAPTER 28

1 The word of the LORD came again unto me, saying,

2 Son of man, say unto the prince of Tyrus, Thus saith the Lord GOD; Because thine heart is lifted up, and thou hast said, I am a God, I sit in the seat of God, in the midst of the seas; yet thou art a man, and not God, though thou set thine heart as the heart of God:

EZEKIEL

3 Behold, thou art wiser than Daniel; there is no secret that they can hide from thee:

4 With thy wisdom and with thine understanding thou hast gotten thee riches, and hast gotten gold and silver into thy treasures:

5 By thy great wisdom and by thy traffick hast thou increased thy riches, and thine heart is lifted up because of thy riches:

6 Therefore thus saith the Lord GOD; Because thou hast set thine heart as the heart of God;

7 Behold, therefore I will bring strangers upon thee, the terrible of the nations: and they shall draw their swords against the beauty of thy wisdom, and they shall defile thy brightness.

8 They shall bring thee down to the pit, and thou shalt die the deaths of them that are slain in the midst of the seas.

EZEKIEL

9 Wilt thou yet say before him that slayeth thee, I am God? but thou shalt be a man, and no God, in the hand of him that slayeth thee.

10 Thou shalt die the deaths of the uncircumcised by the hand of strangers: for I have spoken it, saith the Lord GOD.

11 Moreover the word of the LORD came unto me, saying,

12 Son of man, take up a lamentation upon the king of Tyrus, and say unto him, Thus saith the Lord GOD; Thou sealest up the sum, full of wisdom, and perfect in beauty.

13 Thou hast been in Eden the garden of God; every precious stone was thy covering, the sardius, topaz, and the diamond, the beryl, the onyx, and the jasper, the sapphire, the emerald, and the carbuncle, and gold: the workmanship of thy tabrets and of thy pipes was prepared in thee in the day that thou wast created.

EZEKIEL

14 Thou art the anointed cherub that covereth; and I have set thee so: thou wast upon the holy mountain of God; thou hast walked up and down in the midst of the stones of fire.

15 Thou wast perfect in thy ways from the day that thou wast created, till iniquity was found in thee.

16 By the multitude of thy merchandise they have filled the midst of thee with violence, and thou hast sinned: therefore I will cast thee as profane out of the mountain of God: and I will destroy thee, O covering cherub, from the midst of the stones of fire.

17 Thine heart was lifted up because of thy beauty, thou hast corrupted thy wisdom by reason of thy brightness: I will cast thee to the ground, I will lay thee before kings, that they may behold thee.

EZEKIEL

18 Thou hast defiled thy sanctuaries by the multitude of thine iniquities, by the iniquity of thy traffick; therefore will I bring forth a fire from the midst of thee, it shall devour thee, and I will bring thee to ashes upon the earth in the sight of all them that behold thee.

19 All they that know thee among the people shall be astonished at thee: thou shalt be a terror, and never shalt thou be any more.

20 Again the word of the LORD came unto me, saying,

21 Son of man, set thy face against Zidon, and prophesy against it,

22 And say, Thus saith the Lord GOD; Behold, I am against thee, O Zidon; and I will be glorified in the midst of thee: and they shall know that I am the LORD, when I shall have executed judgments in her, and shall be sanctified in her.

EZEKIEL

23 For I will send into her pestilence, and blood into her streets; and the wounded shall be judged in the midst of her by the sword upon her on every side; and they shall know that I am the LORD.

24 And there shall be no more a pricking brier unto the house of Israel, nor any grieving thorn of all that are round about them, that despised them; and they shall know that I am the Lord GOD.

25 Thus saith the Lord GOD; When I shall have gathered the house of Israel from the people among whom they are scattered, and shall be sanctified in them in the sight of the heathen, then shall they dwell in their land that I have given to my servant Jacob.

26 And they shall dwell safely therein, and shall build houses, and plant vineyards; yea, they shall dwell with confidence, when I have executed judgments upon all those that despise them round about them; and they shall know that I am the LORD their God.

EZEKIEL

CHAPTER 29

1 In the tenth year, in the tenth month, in the twelfth day of the month, the word of the LORD came unto me, saying,

2 Son of man, set thy face against Pharaoh king of Egypt, and prophesy against him, and against all Egypt:

3 Speak, and say, Thus saith the Lord GOD; Behold, I am against thee, Pharaoh king of Egypt, the great dragon that lieth in the midst of his rivers, which hath said, My river is mine own, and I have made it for myself.

4 But I will put hooks in thy jaws, and I will cause the fish of thy rivers to stick unto thy scales, and I will bring thee up out of the midst of thy rivers, and all the fish of thy rivers shall stick unto thy scales.

EZEKIEL

5 And I will leave thee thrown into the wilderness, thee and all the fish of thy rivers: thou shalt fall upon the open fields; thou shalt not be brought together, nor gathered: I have given thee for meat to the beasts of the field and to the fowls of the heaven.

6 And all the inhabitants of Egypt shall know that I am the LORD, because they have been a staff of reed to the house of Israel.

7 When they took hold of thee by thy hand, thou didst break, and rend all their shoulder: and when they leaned upon thee, thou brakest, and madest all their loins to be at a stand.

8 Therefore thus saith the Lord GOD; Behold, I will bring a sword upon thee, and cut off man and beast out of thee.

9 And the land of Egypt shall be desolate and waste; and they shall know that I am the LORD: because he hath said, The river is mine, and I have made it.

EZEKIEL

10 Behold, therefore I am against thee, and against thy rivers, and I will make the land of Egypt utterly waste and desolate, from the tower of Syene even unto the border of Ethiopia.

11 No foot of man shall pass through it, nor foot of beast shall pass through it, neither shall it be inhabited forty years.

12 And I will make the land of Egypt desolate in the midst of the countries that are desolate, and her cities among the cities that are laid waste shall be desolate forty years: and I will scatter the Egyptians among the nations, and will disperse them through the countries.

13 Yet thus saith the Lord GOD; At the end of forty years will I gather the Egyptians from the people whither they were scattered:

14 And I will bring again the captivity of Egypt, and will cause them to return into the land of Pathros, into the land of their habitation; and they shall be there a base kingdom.

EZEKIEL

15 It shall be the basest of the kingdoms; neither shall it exalt itself any more above the nations: for I will diminish them, that they shall no more rule over the nations.

16 And it shall be no more the confidence of the house of Israel, which bringeth their iniquity to remembrance, when they shall look after them: but they shall know that I am the Lord GOD.

17 And it came to pass in the seven and twentieth year, in the first month, in the first day of the month, the word of the LORD came unto me, saying,

18 Son of man, Nebuchadrezzar king of Babylon caused his army to serve a great service against Tyrus: every head was made bald, and every shoulder was peeled: yet had he no wages, nor his army, for Tyrus, for the service that he had served against it:

EZEKIEL

19 Therefore thus saith the Lord GOD; Behold, I will give the land of Egypt unto Nebuchadrezzar king of Babylon; and he shall take her multitude, and take her spoil, and take her prey; and it shall be the wages for his army.

20 I have given him the land of Egypt for his labour wherewith he served against it, because they wrought for me, saith the Lord GOD.

21 In that day will I cause the horn of the house of Israel to bud forth, and I will give thee the opening of the mouth in the midst of them; and they shall know that I am the LORD.

CHAPTER 30

1 The word of the LORD came again unto me, saying,

2 Son of man, prophesy and say, Thus saith the Lord GOD; Howl ye, Woe worth the day!

3 For the day is near, even the day of the LORD is near, a cloudy day; it shall be the time of the heathen.

EZEKIEL

4 And the sword shall come upon Egypt, and great pain shall be in Ethiopia, when the slain shall fall in Egypt, and they shall take away her multitude, and her foundations shall be broken down.

5 Ethiopia, and Libya, and Lydia, and all the mingled people, and Chub, and the men of the land that is in league, shall fall with them by the sword.

6 Thus saith the LORD; They also that uphold Egypt shall fall; and the pride of her power shall come down: from the tower of Syene shall they fall in it by the sword, saith the Lord GOD.

7 And they shall be desolate in the midst of the countries that are desolate, and her cities shall be in the midst of the cities that are wasted.

8 And they shall know that I am the LORD, when I have set a fire in Egypt, and when all her helpers shall be destroyed.

EZEKIEL

9 In that day shall messengers go forth from me in ships to make the careless Ethiopians afraid, and great pain shall come upon them, as in the day of Egypt: for, lo, it cometh.

10 Thus saith the Lord GOD; I will also make the multitude of Egypt to cease by the hand of Nebuchadrezzar king of Babylon.

11 He and his people with him, the terrible of the nations, shall be brought to destroy the land: and they shall draw their swords against Egypt, and fill the land with the slain.

12 And I will make the rivers dry, and sell the land into the hand of the wicked: and I will make the land waste, and all that is therein, by the hand of strangers: I the LORD have spoken it.

13 Thus saith the Lord GOD; I will also destroy the idols, and I will cause their images to cease out of Noph; and there shall be no more a prince of the land of Egypt: and I will put a fear in the land of Egypt.

EZEKIEL

14 And I will make Pathros desolate, and will set fire in Zoan, and will execute judgments in No.

15 And I will pour my fury upon Sin, the strength of Egypt; and I will cut off the multitude of No.

16 And I will set fire in Egypt: Sin shall have great pain, and No shall be rent asunder, and Noph shall have distresses daily.

17 The young men of Aven and of Pi-beseth shall fall by the sword: and these cities shall go into captivity.

18 At Tehaphnehes also the day shall be darkened, when I shall break there the yokes of Egypt: and the pomp of her strength shall cease in her: as for her, a cloud shall cover her, and her daughters shall go into captivity.

19 Thus will I execute judgments in Egypt: and they shall know that I am the LORD.

EZEKIEL

20 And it came to pass in the eleventh year, in the first month, in the seventh day of the month, that the word of the LORD came unto me, saying,

21 Son of man, I have broken the arm of Pharaoh king of Egypt; and, lo, it shall not be bound up to be healed, to put a roller to bind it, to make it strong to hold the sword.

22 Therefore thus saith the Lord GOD; Behold, I am against Pharaoh king of Egypt, and will break his arms, the strong, and that which was broken; and I will cause the sword to fall out of his hand.

23 And I will scatter the Egyptians among the nations, and will disperse them through the countries.

24 And I will strengthen the arms of the king of Babylon, and put my sword in his hand: but I will break Pharaoh's arms, and he shall groan before him with the groanings of a deadly wounded man.

EZEKIEL

25. But I will strengthen the arms of the king of
Babylon, and the arms of Pharaoh shall fall down; and
they shall know that I am the LORD, when I shall put
my sword into the hand of the king of Babylon, and he
shall stretch it out upon the land of Egypt.
26. And I will scatter the Egyptians among the
nations, and disperse them among the countries; and
they shall know that I am the LORD.

CHAPTER 31
1. And it came to pass in the eleventh year, in the
third month, in the first day of the month, that the
word of the LORD came unto me, saying,
2. Son of man, speak unto Pharaoh king of Egypt, and
to his multitude; Whom art thou like in thy greatness?

3 Behold, the Assyrian was a cedar in Lebanon with fair branches, and with a shadowing shroud, and of an high stature; and his top was among the thick boughs.

4 The waters made him great; the deep set him up on high with her rivers running round about his plants, and sent out her little rivers unto all the trees of the field.

5 Therefore his height was exalted above all the trees of the field, and his boughs were multiplied, and his branches became long because of the multitude of waters, when he shot forth.

6 All the fowls of heaven made their nests in his boughs, and under his branches did all the beasts of the field bring forth their young, and under his shadow dwelt all great nations.

7 Thus was he fair in his greatness, in the length of his branches: for his root was by great waters.

EZEKIEL

8 The cedars in the garden of God could not hide him: the fir trees were not like his boughs, and the chestnut trees were not like his branches; nor any tree in the garden of God was like unto him in his beauty.

9 I have made him fair by the multitude of his branches: so that all the trees of Eden, that were in the garden of God, envied him.

10 Therefore thus saith the Lord GOD; Because thou hast lifted up thyself in height, and he hath shot up his top among the thick boughs, and his heart is lifted up in his height;

11 I have therefore delivered him into the hand of the mighty one of the heathen; he shall surely deal with him: I have driven him out for his wickedness.

EZEKIEL

12 And strangers, the terrible of the nations, have cut him off, and have left him: upon the mountains and in all the valleys his branches are fallen, and his boughs are broken by all the rivers of the land; and all the people of the earth are gone down from his shadow, and have left him.

13 Upon his ruin shall all the fowls of the heaven remain, and all the beasts of the field shall be upon his branches:

14 To the end that none of all the trees by the waters exalt themselves for their height, neither shoot up their top among the thick boughs, neither their trees stand up in their height, all that drink water: for they are all delivered unto death, to the nether parts of the earth, in the midst of the children of men, with them that go down to the pit.

EZEKIEL

15 Thus saith the Lord GOD; In the day when he went down to the grave I caused a mourning: I covered the deep for him, and I restrained the floods thereof, and the great waters were stayed: and I caused Lebanon to mourn for him, and all the trees of the field fainted for him.

16 I made the nations to shake at the sound of his fall, when I cast him down to hell with them that descend into the pit: and all the trees of Eden, the choice and best of Lebanon, all that drink water, shall be comforted in the nether parts of the earth.

17 They also went down into hell with him unto them that be slain with the sword; and they that were his arm, that dwelt under his shadow in the midst of the heathen.

EZEKIEL

18 To whom art thou thus like in glory and in greatness among the trees of Eden? yet shalt thou be brought down with the trees of Eden unto the nether parts of the earth: thou shalt lie in the midst of the uncircumcised with them that be slain by the sword. This is Pharaoh and all his multitude, saith the Lord GOD.

CHAPTER 32

1 And it came to pass in the twelfth year, in the twelfth month, in the first day of the month, that the word of the LORD came unto me, saying,

2 Son of man, take up a lamentation for Pharaoh king of Egypt, and say unto him, Thou art like a young lion of the nations, and thou art as a whale in the seas: and thou camest forth with thy rivers, and troubledst the waters with thy feet, and fouledst their rivers.

3 Thus saith the Lord GOD; I will therefore spread out my net over thee with a company of many people; and they shall bring thee up in my net.

EZEKIEL

4 Then will I leave thee upon the land, I will cast thee forth upon the open field, and will cause all the fowls of the heaven to remain upon thee, and I will fill the beasts of the whole earth with thee.

5 And I will lay thy flesh upon the mountains, and fill the valleys with thy height.

6 I will also water with thy blood the land wherein thou swimmest, even to the mountains; and the rivers shall be full of thee.

7 And when I shall put thee out, I will cover the heaven, and make the stars thereof dark; I will cover the sun with a cloud, and the moon shall not give her light.

8 All the bright lights of heaven will I make dark over thee, and set darkness upon thy land, saith the Lord GOD.

9 I will also vex the hearts of many people, when I shall bring thy destruction among the nations, into the countries which thou hast not known.

EZEKIEL

10 Yea, I will make many people amazed at thee, and their kings shall be horribly afraid for thee, when I shall brandish my sword before them; and they shall tremble at every moment, every man for his own life, in the day of thy fall.

11 For thus saith the Lord GOD; The sword of the king of Babylon shall come upon thee.

12 By the swords of the mighty will I cause thy multitude to fall, the terrible of the nations, all of them: and they shall spoil the pomp of Egypt, and all the multitude thereof shall be destroyed.

13 I will destroy also all the beasts thereof from beside the great waters; neither shall the foot of man trouble them any more, nor the hoofs of beasts trouble them.

14 Then will I make their waters deep, and cause their rivers to run like oil, saith the Lord GOD.

EZEKIEL

15 When I shall make the land of Egypt desolate, and the country shall be destitute of that whereof it was full, when I shall smite all them that dwell therein, then shall they know that I am the LORD.

16 This is the lamentation wherewith they shall lament her: the daughters of the nations shall lament her: they shall lament for her, even for Egypt, and for all her multitude, saith the Lord GOD.

17 It came to pass also in the twelfth year, in the fifteenth day of the month, that the word of the LORD came unto me, saying,

18 Son of man, wail for the multitude of Egypt, and cast them down, even her, and the daughters of the famous nations, unto the nether parts of the earth, with them that go down into the pit.

19 Whom dost thou pass in beauty? go down, and be thou laid with the uncircumcised.

EZEKIEL

20 They shall fall in the midst of them that are slain by the sword: she is delivered to the sword: draw her and all her multitudes.

21 The strong among the mighty shall speak to him out of the midst of hell with them that help him: they are gone down, they lie uncircumcised, slain by the sword.

22 Asshur is there and all her company: his graves are about him: all of them slain, fallen by the sword:

23 Whose graves are set in the sides of the pit, and her company is round about her grave: all of them slain, fallen by the sword, which caused terror in the land of the living.

24 There is Elam and all her multitude round about her grave, all of them slain, fallen by the sword, which are gone down uncircumcised into the nether parts of the earth, which caused their terror in the land of the living; yet have they borne their shame with them that go down to the pit.

EZEKIEL

25 They have set her a bed in the midst of the slain with all her multitude: her graves are round about him: all of them uncircumcised, slain by the sword: though their terror was caused in the land of the living, yet have they borne their shame with them that go down to the pit: he is put in the midst of them that be slain.

26 There is Meshech, Tubal, and all her multitude: her graves are round about him: all of them uncircumcised, slain by the sword, though they caused their terror in the land of the living.

27 And they shall not lie with the mighty that are fallen of the uncircumcised, which are gone down to hell with their weapons of war: and they have laid their swords under their heads, but their iniquities shall be upon their bones, though they were the terror of the mighty in the land of the living.

EZEKIEL

28 Yea, thou shalt be broken in the midst of the uncircumcised, and shalt lie with them that are slain with the sword.

29 There is Edom, her kings, and all her princes, which with their might are laid by them that were slain by the sword: they shall lie with the uncircumcised, and with them that go down to the pit.

30 There be the princes of the north, all of them, and all the Zidonians, which are gone down with the slain; with their terror they are ashamed of their might; and they lie uncircumcised with them that be slain by the sword, and bear their shame with them that go down to the pit.

31 Pharaoh shall see them, and shall be comforted over all his multitude, even Pharaoh and all his army slain by the sword, saith the Lord GOD.

EZEKIEL

32 For I have caused my terror in the land of the living: and he shall be laid in the midst of the uncircumcised with them that are slain with the sword, even Pharaoh and all his multitude, saith the Lord GOD.

CHAPTER 33

1 Again the word of the LORD came unto me, saying,

2 Son of man, speak to the children of thy people, and say unto them, When I bring the sword upon a land, if the people of the land take a man of their coasts, and set him for their watchman:

3 If when he seeth the sword come upon the land, he blow the trumpet, and warn the people;

4 Then whosoever heareth the sound of the trumpet, and taketh not warning; if the sword come, and take him away, his blood shall be upon his own head.

EZEKIEL

5 He heard the sound of the trumpet, and took not warning; his blood shall be upon him. But he that taketh warning shall deliver his soul.

6 But if the watchman see the sword come, and blow not the trumpet, and the people be not warned; if the sword come, and take any person from among them, he is taken away in his iniquity; but his blood will I require at the watchman's hand.

7 So thou, O son of man, I have set thee a watchman unto the house of Israel; therefore thou shalt hear the word at my mouth, and warn them from me.

8 When I say unto the wicked, O wicked man, thou shalt surely die; if thou dost not speak to warn the wicked from his way, that wicked man shall die in his iniquity; but his blood will I require at thine hand.

EZEKIEL

9 Nevertheless, if thou warn the wicked of his way to turn from it; if he do not turn from his way, he shall die in his iniquity; but thou hast delivered thy soul.

10 Therefore, O thou son of man, speak unto the house of Israel; Thus ye speak, saying, If our transgressions and our sins be upon us, and we pine away in them, how should we then live?

11 Say unto them, As I live, saith the Lord GOD, I have no pleasure in the death of the wicked; but that the wicked turn from his way and live: turn ye, turn ye from your evil ways; for why will ye die, O house of Israel?

12 Therefore, thou son of man, say unto the children of thy people, The righteousness of the righteous shall not deliver him in the day of his transgression: as for the wickedness of the wicked, he shall not fall thereby in the day that he turneth from his wickedness; neither shall the righteous be able to live for his righteousness in the day that he sinneth.

EZEKIEL

13 When I shall say to the righteous, that he shall surely live; if he trust to his own righteousness, and commit iniquity, all his righteousnesses shall not be remembered; but for his iniquity that he hath committed, he shall die for it.

14 Again, when I say unto the wicked, Thou shalt surely die; if he turn from his sin, and do that which is lawful and right;

15 If the wicked restore the pledge, give again that he had robbed, walk in the statutes of life, without committing iniquity; he shall surely live, he shall not die.

16 None of his sins that he hath committed shall be mentioned unto him: he hath done that which is lawful and right; he shall surely live.

17 Yet the children of thy people say, The way of the Lord is not equal: but as for them, their way is not equal.

18 When the righteous turneth from his righteousness, and committeth iniquity, he shall even die thereby.

EZEKIEL

19 But if the wicked turn from his wickedness, and do that which is lawful and right, he shall live thereby.

20 Yet ye say, The way of the Lord is not equal. O ye house of Israel, I will judge you every one after his ways.

21 And it came to pass in the twelfth year of our captivity, in the tenth month, in the fifth day of the month, that one that had escaped out of Jerusalem came unto me, saying, The city is smitten.

22 Now the hand of the LORD was upon me in the evening, afore he that was escaped came; and had opened my mouth, until he came to me in the morning; and my mouth was opened, and I was no more dumb.

23 Then the word of the LORD came unto me, saying,

EZEKIEL

24 Son of man, they that inhabit those wastes of the land of Israel speak, saying, Abraham was one, and he inherited the land: but we are many; the land is given us for inheritance.

25 Wherefore say unto them, Thus saith the Lord GOD; Ye eat with the blood, and lift up your eyes toward your idols, and shed blood: and shall ye possess the land?

26 Ye stand upon your sword, ye work abomination, and ye defile every one his neighbour's wife: and shall ye possess the land?

27 Say thou thus unto them, Thus saith the Lord GOD; As I live, surely they that are in the wastes shall fall by the sword, and him that is in the open field will I give to the beasts to be devoured, and they that be in the forts and in the caves shall die of the pestilence.

EZEKIEL

28 for I will lay the land most desolate, and the pomp of her strength shall cease; and the mountains of Israel shall be desolate, that none shall pass through.

29 Then shall they know that I am the LORD, when I have laid the land most desolate because of all their abominations which they have committed.

30 Also, thou son of man, the children of thy people still are talking against thee by the walls and in the doors of the houses, and speak one to another, every one to his brother, saying, Come, I pray you, and hear what is the word that cometh forth from the LORD.

31 And they come unto thee as the people cometh, and they sit before thee as my people, and they hear thy words, but they will not do them: for with their mouth they shew much love, but their heart goeth after their covetousness.

EZEKIEL

32 And, lo, thou art unto them as a very lovely song of one that hath a pleasant voice, and can play well on an instrument: for they hear thy words, but they do them not.

33 And when this cometh to pass, (lo, it will come,) then shall they know that a prophet hath been among them.

CHAPTER 34

1 And the word of the LORD came unto me, saying,

2 Son of man, prophesy against the shepherds of Israel, prophesy, and say unto them, Thus saith the Lord GOD unto the shepherds; Woe be to the shepherds of Israel that do feed themselves! should not the shepherds feed the flocks?

3 Ye eat the fat, and ye clothe you with the wool, ye kill them that are fed: but ye feed not the flock.

EZEKIEL

4 The diseased have ye not strengthened, neither have ye healed that which was sick, neither have ye bound up that which was broken, neither have ye brought again that which was driven away, neither have ye sought that which was lost; but with force and with cruelty have ye ruled them.

5 And they were scattered, because there is no shepherd: and they became meat to all the beasts of the field, when they were scattered.

6 My sheep wandered through all the mountains, and upon every high hill: yea, my flock was scattered upon all the face of the earth, and none did search or seek after them.

7 Therefore, ye shepherds, hear the word of the LORD;

8 As I live, saith the Lord GOD, surely because my flock became a prey, and my flock became meat to every beast of the field, because there was no shepherd, neither did my shepherds search for my flock, but the shepherds fed themselves, and fed not my flock;

EZEKIEL

9 Therefore, O ye shepherds, hear the word of the LORD;

10 Thus saith the Lord GOD; Behold, I am against the shepherds; and I will require my flock at their hand, and cause them to cease from feeding the flock; neither shall the shepherds feed themselves any more; for I will deliver my flock from their mouth, that they may not be meat for them.

11 For thus saith the Lord GOD; Behold, I, even I, will both search my sheep, and seek them out.

12 As a shepherd seeketh out his flock in the day that he is among his sheep that are scattered; so will I seek out my sheep, and will deliver them out of all places where they have been scattered in the cloudy and dark day.

13 And I will bring them out from the people, and gather them from the countries, and will bring them to their own land, and feed them upon the mountains of Israel by the rivers, and in all the inhabited places of the country.

EZEKIEL

14 I will feed them in a good pasture, and upon the high mountains of Israel shall their fold be: there shall they lie in a good fold, and in a fat pasture shall they feed upon the mountains of Israel.

15 I will feed my flock, and I will cause them to lie down, saith the Lord GOD.

16 I will seek that which was lost, and bring again that which was driven away, and will bind up that which was broken, and will strengthen that which was sick: but I will destroy the fat and the strong; I will feed them with judgment.

17 And as for you, O my flock, thus saith the Lord GOD; Behold, I judge between cattle and cattle, between the rams and the he goats.

18 Seemeth it a small thing unto you to have eaten up the good pasture, but ye must tread down with your feet the residue of your pastures? and to have drunk of the deep waters, but ye must foul the residue with your feet?

19 And as for my flock, they eat that which ye have trodden with your feet; and they drink that which ye have fouled with your feet.

20 Therefore thus saith the Lord GOD unto them; Behold, I, even I, will judge between the fat cattle and between the lean cattle.

21 Because ye have thrust with side and with shoulder, and pushed all the diseased with your horns, till ye have scattered them abroad;

22 Therefore will I save my flock, and they shall no more be a prey; and I will judge between cattle and cattle.

23 And I will set up one shepherd over them, and he shall feed them, even my servant David; he shall feed them, and he shall be their shepherd.

24 And I the LORD will be their God, and my servant David a prince among them; I the LORD have spoken it.

EZEKIEL

25 And I will make with them a covenant of peace, and will cause the evil beasts to cease out of the land: and they shall dwell safely in the wilderness, and sleep in the woods.

26 And I will make them and the places round about my hill a blessing; and I will cause the shower to come down in his season; there shall be showers of blessing.

27 And the tree of the field shall yield her fruit, and the earth shall yield her increase, and they shall be safe in their land, and shall know that I am the LORD, when I have broken the bands of their yoke, and delivered them out of the hand of those that served themselves of them.

28 And they shall no more be a prey to the heathen, neither shall the beast of the land devour them; but they shall dwell safely, and none shall make them afraid.

29 And I will raise up for them a plant of renown, and they shall be no more consumed with hunger in the land, neither bear the shame of the heathen any more.

30 Thus shall they know that I the LORD their God am with them, and that they, even the house of Israel, are my people, saith the Lord GOD.

31 And ye my flock, the flock of my pasture, are men, and I am your God, saith the Lord GOD.

CHAPTER 35

1 Moreover the word of the LORD came unto me, saying,

2 Son of man, set thy face against mount Seir, and prophesy against it,

3 And say unto it, Thus saith the Lord GOD; Behold, O mount Seir, I am against thee, and I will stretch out mine hand against thee, and I will make thee most desolate.

EZEKIEL

4 I will lay thy cities waste, and thou shalt be
desolate, and thou shalt know that I am the LORD.
5 Because thou hast had a perpetual hatred, and
hast shed the blood of the children of Israel by the
force of the sword in the time of their calamity, in the
time that their iniquity had an end:
6 Therefore, as I live, saith the Lord GOD, I will
prepare thee unto blood, and blood shall pursue thee:
sith thou hast not hated blood, even blood shall pursue
thee.
7 Thus will I make mount Seir most desolate, and cut
off from it him that passeth out and him that
returneth.
8 And I will fill his mountains with his slain men: in thy
hills, and in thy valleys, and in all thy rivers, shall they
fall that are slain with the sword.
9 I will make thee perpetual desolations, and thy cities
shall not return: and ye shall know that I am the
LORD.

EZEKIEL

10 Because thou hast said, These two nations and these two countries shall be mine, and we will possess it; whereas the LORD was there:

11 Therefore, as I live, saith the Lord GOD, I will even do according to thine anger, and according to thine envy which thou hast used out of thy hatred against them; and I will make myself known among them, when I have judged thee.

12 And thou shalt know that I am the LORD, and that I have heard all thy blasphemies which thou hast spoken against the mountains of Israel, saying, They are laid desolate, they are given us to consume.

13 Thus with your mouth ye have boasted against me, and have multiplied your words against me: I have heard them.

14 Thus saith the Lord GOD; When the whole earth rejoiceth, I will make thee desolate.

EZEKIEL

15 As thou didst rejoice at the inheritance of the house of Israel, because it was desolate, so will I do unto thee: thou shalt be desolate, O mount Seir, and all Idumea, even all of it: and they shall know that I am the LORD.

CHAPTER 36

1 Also, thou son of man, prophesy unto the mountains of Israel, and say, Ye mountains of Israel, hear the word of the LORD:

2 Thus saith the Lord GOD; Because the enemy hath said against you, Aha, even the ancient high places are ours in possession:

3 Therefore prophesy and say, Thus saith the Lord GOD; Because they have made you desolate, and swallowed you up on every side, that ye might be a possession unto the residue of the heathen, and ye are taken up in the lips of talkers, and are an infamy of the people:

EZEKIEL

4 Therefore, ye mountains of Israel, hear the word of the Lord GOD; Thus saith the Lord GOD to the mountains, and to the hills, to the rivers, and to the valleys, to the desolate wastes, and to the cities that are forsaken, which became a prey and derision to the residue of the heathen that are round about;

5 Therefore thus saith the Lord GOD; Surely in the fire of my jealousy have I spoken against the residue of the heathen, and against all Idumea, which have appointed my land into their possession with the joy of all their heart, with despiteful minds, to cast it out for a prey.

6 Prophesy therefore concerning the land of Israel, and say unto the mountains, and to the hills, to the rivers, and to the valleys, Thus saith the Lord GOD; Behold, I have spoken in my jealousy and in my fury, because ye have borne the shame of the heathen:

EZEKIEL

7 Therefore thus saith the Lord GOD; I have lifted up mine hand, Surely the heathen that are about you, they shall bear their shame.

8 But ye, O mountains of Israel, ye shall shoot forth your branches, and yield your fruit to my people of Israel; for they are at hand to come.

9 For, behold, I am for you, and I will turn unto you, and ye shall be tilled and sown:

10 And I will multiply men upon you, all the house of Israel, even all of it: and the cities shall be inhabited, and the wastes shall be builded:

11 And I will multiply upon you man and beast; and they shall increase and bring fruit: and I will settle you after your old estates, and will do better unto you than at your beginnings: and ye shall know that I am the LORD.

EZEKIEL

2 Yea, I will cause man to walk upon you, even my people Israel; and they shall possess thee, and thou shalt be their inheritance, and thou shalt no more henceforth bereave them of men.

3 Thus saith the Lord GOD; Because they say unto you, Thou land devourest up men, and hast bereaved thy nations;

4 Therefore thou shalt devour men no more, neither bereave thy nations any more, saith the Lord GOD.

5 Neither will I cause men to hear in thee the shame of the heathen any more, neither shalt thou bear the reproach of the people any more, neither shalt thou cause thy nations to fall any more, saith the Lord GOD.

6 Moreover the word of the LORD came unto me, saying,

EZEKIEL

17 Son of man, when the house of Israel dwelt in their own land, they defiled it by their own way and by their doings: their way was before me as the uncleanness of a removed woman.

18 Wherefore I poured my fury upon them for the blood that they had shed upon the land, and for their idols wherewith they had polluted it:

19 And I scattered them among the heathen, and they were dispersed through the countries: according to their way and according to their doings I judged them.

20 And when they entered unto the heathen, whither they went, they profaned my holy name, when they said to them, These are the people of the LORD, and are gone forth out of his land.

21 But I had pity for mine holy name, which the house of Israel had profaned among the heathen, whither they went.

EZEKIEL

22 Therefore say unto the house of Israel, Thus saith the Lord GOD; I do not this for your sakes, O house of Israel, but for mine holy name's sake, which ye have profaned among the heathen, whither ye went.

23 And I will sanctify my great name, which was profaned among the heathen, which ye have profaned in the midst of them; and the heathen shall know that I am the LORD, saith the Lord GOD, when I shall be sanctified in you before their eyes.

24 For I will take you from among the heathen, and gather you out of all countries, and will bring you into your own land.

25 Then will I sprinkle clean water upon you, and ye shall be clean: from all your filthiness, and from all your idols, will I cleanse you.

26 A new heart also will I give you, and a new spirit will I put within you: and I will take away the stony heart out of your flesh, and I will give you an heart of flesh.

EZEKIEL

27- And I will put my spirit within you, and cause you to walk in my statutes, and ye shall keep my judgments, and do them.

28- And ye shall dwell in the land that I gave to your fathers; and ye shall be my people, and I will be your God.

29- I will also save you from all your uncleannesses: and I will call for the corn, and will increase it, and lay no famine upon you.

30- And I will multiply the fruit of the tree, and the increase of the field, that ye shall receive no more reproach of famine among the heathen.

31- Then shall ye remember your own evil ways, and your doings that were not good, and shall lothe yourselves in your own sight for your iniquities and for your abominations.

32- Not for your sakes do I this, saith the Lord GOD, be it known unto you: be ashamed and confounded for your own ways, O house of Israel.

EZEKIEL

33 Thus saith the Lord GOD; In the day that I shall have cleansed you from all your iniquities I will also cause you to dwell in the cities, and the wastes shall be builded.

34 And the desolate land shall be tilled, whereas it lay desolate in the sight of all that passed by.

35 And they shall say, This land that was desolate is become like the garden of Eden; and the waste and desolate and ruined cities are become fenced, and are inhabited.

36 Then the heathen that are left round about you shall know that I the LORD build the ruined places, and plant that that was desolate: I the LORD have spoken it, and I will do it.

37 Thus saith the Lord GOD; I will yet for this be enquired of by the house of Israel, to do it for them; I will increase them with men like a flock.

EZEKIEL

38 As the holy flock, as the flock of Jerusalem in her solemn feasts; so shall the waste cities be filled with flocks of men: and they shall know that I am the LORD.

CHAPTER 37

1 The hand of the LORD was upon me, and carried me out in the spirit of the LORD, and set me down in the midst of the valley which was full of bones,

2 And caused me to pass by them round about: and, behold, there were very many in the open valley; and, lo, they were very dry.

3 And he said unto me, Son of man, can these bones live? And I answered, O Lord GOD, thou knowest.

4 Again he said unto me, Prophesy upon these bones, and say unto them, O ye dry bones, hear the word of the LORD.

EZEKIEL

5 Thus saith the Lord GOD unto these bones; Behold, I will cause breath to enter into you, and ye shall live:

6 And I will lay sinews upon you, and will bring up flesh upon you, and cover you with skin, and put breath in you, and ye shall live; and ye shall know that I am the LORD.

7 So I prophesied as I was commanded: and as I prophesied, there was a noise, and behold a shaking, and the bones came together, bone to his bone.

8 And when I beheld, lo, the sinews and the flesh came up upon them, and the skin covered them above: but there was no breath in them.

9 Then said he unto me, Prophesy unto the wind, prophesy, son of man, and say to the wind, Thus saith the Lord GOD; Come from the four winds, O breath, and breathe upon these slain, that they may live.

EZEKIEL

10 So I prophesied as he commanded me, and the breath came into them, and they lived, and stood up upon their feet, an exceeding great army.

11 Then he said unto me, Son of man, these bones are the whole house of Israel: behold, they say, Our bones are dried, and our hope is lost: we are cut off for our parts.

12 Therefore prophesy and say unto them, Thus saith the Lord GOD; Behold, O my people, I will open your graves, and cause you to come up out of your graves, and bring you into the land of Israel.

13 And ye shall know that I am the LORD, when I have opened your graves, O my people, and brought you up out of your graves,

14 And shall put my spirit in you, and ye shall live, and I shall place you in your own land: then shall ye know that I the LORD have spoken it, and performed it, saith the LORD.

EZEKIEL

15   The word of the LORD came again unto me, saying,

16 Moreover, thou son of man, take thee one stick, and write upon it, For Judah, and for the children of Israel his companions: then take another stick, and write upon it, For Joseph, the stick of Ephraim, and for all the house of Israel his companions:

17 And join them one to another into one stick; and they shall become one in thine hand.

18   And when the children of thy people shall speak unto thee, saying, Wilt thou not shew us what thou meanest by these?

19 Say unto them, Thus saith the Lord GOD; Behold, I will take the stick of Joseph, which is in the hand of Ephraim, and the tribes of Israel his fellows, and will put them with him, even with the stick of Judah, and make them one stick, and they shall be one in mine hand.

EZEKIEL

20 - And the sticks whereon thou writest shall be in thine hand before their eyes.

21 - And say unto them, Thus saith the Lord GOD; Behold, I will take the children of Israel from among the heathen, whither they be gone, and will gather them on every side, and bring them into their own land:

22 - And I will make them one nation in the land upon the mountains of Israel; and one king shall be king to them all: and they shall be no more two nations, neither shall they be divided into two kingdoms any more at all:

23 - Neither shall they defile themselves any more with their idols, nor with their detestable things, nor with any of their transgressions: but I will save them out of all their dwellingplaces, wherein they have sinned, and will cleanse them: so shall they be my people, and I will be their God.

EZEKIEL

24- And David my servant shall be king over them;
and they all shall have one shepherd: they shall also
walk in my judgments, and observe my statutes, and
do them.

25- And they shall dwell in the land that I have given
unto Jacob my servant, wherein your fathers have
dwelt; and they shall dwell therein, even they, and
their children, and their children's children for ever:
and my servant David shall be their prince for ever.

26- Moreover I will make a covenant of peace with
them; it shall be an everlasting covenant with them:
and I will place them, and multiply them, and will set
my sanctuary in the midst of them for evermore.

27- My tabernacle also shall be with them: yea, I will
be their God, and they shall be my people.

28- And the heathen shall know that I the LORD do
sanctify Israel, when my sanctuary shall be in the
midst of them for evermore.

EZEKIEL

CHAPTER 38

1 And the word of the LORD came unto me, saying,

2 Son of man, set thy face against Gog, the land of Magog, the chief prince of Meshech and Tubal, and prophesy against him,

3 And say, Thus saith the Lord GOD; Behold, I am against thee, O Gog, the chief prince of Meshech and Tubal:

4 And I will turn thee back, and put hooks into thy jaws, and I will bring thee forth, and all thine army, horses and horsemen, all of them clothed with all sorts of armour, even a great company with bucklers and shields, all of them handling swords:

5 Persia, Ethiopia, and Libya with them; all of them with shield and helmet:

6 Gomer, and all his bands; the house of Togarmah of the north quarters, and all his bands: and many people with thee.

EZEKIEL

7 Be thou prepared, and prepare for thyself, thou, and all thy company that are assembled unto thee, and be thou a guard unto them.

8 After many days thou shalt be visited: in the latter years thou shalt come into the land that is brought back from the sword, and is gathered out of many people, against the mountains of Israel, which have been always waste: but it is brought forth out of the nations, and they shall dwell safely all of them.

9 Thou shalt ascend and come like a storm, thou shalt be like a cloud to cover the land, thou, and all thy bands, and many people with thee.

10 Thus saith the Lord GOD; It shall also come to pass, that at the same time shall things come into thy mind, and thou shalt think an evil thought:

EZEKIEL

1 And thou shalt say, I will go up to the land of unwalled villages; I will go to them that are at rest, that dwell safely, all of them dwelling without walls, and having neither bars nor gates,

2 To take a spoil, and to take a prey; to turn thine hand upon the desolate places that are now inhabited, and upon the people that are gathered out of the nations, which have gotten cattle and goods, that dwell in the midst of the land.

3 Sheba, and Dedan, and the merchants of Tarshish, with all the young lions thereof, shall say unto thee, Art thou come to take a spoil? hast thou gathered thy company to take a prey? to carry away silver and gold, to take away cattle and goods, to take a great spoil?

4 Therefore, son of man, prophesy and say unto Gog, Thus saith the Lord GOD; In that day when my people of Israel dwelleth safely, shalt thou not know it?

EZEKIEL

15 And thou shalt come from thy place out of the north parts, thou, and many people with thee, all of them riding upon horses, a great company, and a mighty army:

16 And thou shalt come up against my people of Israel, as a cloud to cover the land; it shall be in the latter days, and I will bring thee against my land, that the heathen may know me, when I shall be sanctified in thee, O Gog, before their eyes.

17 Thus saith the Lord GOD; Art thou he of whom I have spoken in old time by my servants the prophets of Israel, which prophesied in those days many years that I would bring thee against them?

18 And it shall come to pass at the same time when Gog shall come against the land of Israel, saith the Lord GOD, that my fury shall come up in my face.

19 For in my jealousy and in the fire of my wrath have I spoken. Surely in that day there shall be a great shaking in the land of Israel;

20 So that the fishes of the sea, and the fowls of the heaven, and the beasts of the field, and all creeping things that creep upon the earth, and all the men that are upon the face of the earth, shall shake at my presence, and the mountains shall be thrown down, and the steep places shall fall, and every wall shall fall to the ground.

21 And I will call for a sword against him throughout all my mountains, saith the Lord GOD: every man's sword shall be against his brother.

22 And I will plead against him with pestilence and with blood; and I will rain upon him, and upon his bands, and upon the many people that are with him, an overflowing rain, and great hailstones, fire, and brimstone.

23 Thus will I magnify myself, and sanctify myself; and I will be known in the eyes of many nations, and they shall know that I am the LORD.

EZEKIEL

CHAPTER 39

1 Therefore, thou son of man, prophesy against Gog, and say, Thus saith the Lord GOD; Behold, I am against thee, O Gog, the chief prince of Meshech and Tubal:

2 And I will turn thee back, and leave but the sixth part of thee, and will cause thee to come up from the north parts, and will bring thee upon the mountains of Israel:

3 And I will smite thy bow out of thy left hand, and will cause thine arrows to fall out of thy right hand.

4 Thou shalt fall upon the mountains of Israel, thou, and all thy bands, and the people that is with thee: I will give thee unto the ravenous birds of every sort, and to the beasts of the field to be devoured.

5 Thou shalt fall upon the open field: for I have spoken it, saith the Lord GOD.

EZEKIEL

6 - And I will send a fire on Magog, and among them that dwell carelessly in the isles: and they shall know that I am the LORD.

7 - So will I make my holy name known in the midst of my people Israel; and I will not let them pollute my holy name any more: and the heathen shall know that I am the LORD, the Holy One in Israel.

8 - Behold, it is come, and it is done, saith the Lord GOD; this is the day whereof I have spoken.

9 - And they that dwell in the cities of Israel shall go forth, and shall set on fire and burn the weapons, both the shields and the bucklers, the bows and the arrows, and the handstaves, and the spears, and they shall burn them with fire seven years:

10 - So that they shall take no wood out of the field, neither cut down any out of the forests; for they shall burn the weapons with fire: and they shall spoil those that spoiled them, and rob those that robbed them, saith the Lord GOD.

EZEKIEL

11 - And it shall come to pass in that day, that I will give unto Gog a place there of graves in Israel, the valley of the passengers on the east of the sea: and it shall stop the noses of the passengers: and there shall they bury Gog and all his multitude: and they shall call it The valley of Hamon-gog.

12 - And seven months shall the house of Israel be burying of them, that they may cleanse the land.

13 - Yea, all the people of the land shall bury them; and it shall be to them a renown the day that I shall be glorified, saith the Lord GOD.

14 - And they shall sever out men of continual employment, passing through the land to bury with the passengers those that remain upon the face of the earth, to cleanse it: after the end of seven months shall they search.

EZEKIEL

15 And the passengers that pass through the land, when any seeth a man's bone, then shall he set up a sign by it, till the buriers have buried it in the valley of Hamon-gog.

16 And also the name of the city shall be Hamonah. Thus shall they cleanse the land.

17 And, thou son of man, thus saith the Lord GOD; Speak unto every feathered fowl, and to every beast of the field, Assemble yourselves, and come; gather yourselves on every side to my sacrifice that I do sacrifice for you, even a great sacrifice upon the mountains of Israel, that ye may eat flesh, and drink blood.

18 Ye shall eat the flesh of the mighty, and drink the blood of the princes of the earth, of rams, of lambs, and of goats, of bullocks, all of them fatlings of Bashan.

EZEKIEL

19 And ye shall eat fat till ye be full, and drink blood till ye be drunken, of my sacrifice which I have sacrificed for you.

20 Thus ye shall be filled at my table with horses and chariots, with mighty men, and with all men of war, saith the Lord GOD.

21 And I will set my glory among the heathen, and all the heathen shall see my judgment that I have executed, and my hand that I have laid upon them.

22 So the house of Israel shall know that I am the LORD their God from that day and forward.

23 And the heathen shall know that the house of Israel went into captivity for their iniquity: because they trespassed against me, therefore hid I my face from them, and gave them into the hand of their enemies: so fell they all by the sword.

24 According to their uncleanness and according to their transgressions have I done unto them, and hid my face from them.

EZEKIEL

25 Therefore thus saith the Lord GOD; Now will I bring again the captivity of Jacob, and have mercy upon the whole house of Israel, and will be jealous for my holy name;

26 After that they have borne their shame, and all their trespasses whereby they have trespassed against me, when they dwelt safely in their land, and none made them afraid.

27 When I have brought them again from the people, and gathered them out of their enemies' lands, and am sanctified in them in the sight of many nations;

28 Then shall they know that I am the LORD their God, which caused them to be led into captivity among the heathen: but I have gathered them unto their own land, and have left none of them any more there.

29 Neither will I hide my face any more from them: for I have poured out my spirit upon the house of Israel, saith the Lord GOD.

EZEKIEL

CHAPTER 40

In the five and twentieth year of our captivity, in
the beginning of the year, in the tenth day of the
month, in the fourteenth year after that the city was
smitten, in the selfsame day the hand of the LORD
was upon me, and brought me thither.

2 In the visions of God brought he me into the land of
Israel, and set me upon a very high mountain, by which
was as the frame of a city on the south.

3 And he brought me thither, and, behold, there was
a man, whose appearance was like the appearance of
brass, with a line of flax in his hand, and a measuring
reed; and he stood in the gate.

4 And the man said unto me, Son of man, behold with
thine eyes, and hear with thine ears, and set thine
heart upon all that I shall shew thee; for to the intent
that I might shew them unto thee art thou brought
hither: declare all that thou seest to the house of
Israel.

EZEKIEL

5 And behold a wall on the outside of the house round about, and in the mans hand a measuring reed of six cubits long by the cubit and an hand breadth: so he measured the breadth of the building, one reed; and the height, one reed.

6 Then came he unto the gate which looketh toward the east, and went up the stairs thereof, and measured the threshold of the gate, which was one reed broad; and the other threshold of the gate, which was one reed broad.

7 And every little chamber was one reed long, and one reed broad; and between the little chambers were five cubits; and the threshold of the gate by the porch of the gate within was one reed.

8 He measured also the porch of the gate within, one reed.

9 Then measured he the porch of the gate, eight cubits; and the posts thereof, two cubits; and the porch of the gate was inward.

EZEKIEL

10 - And the little chambers of the gate eastward were three on this side, and three on that side; they three were of one measure: and the posts had one measure on this side and on that side.

11 - And he measured the breadth of the entry of the gate, ten cubits; and the length of the gate, thirteen cubits.

12 - The space also before the little chambers was one cubit on this side, and the space was one cubit on that side: and the little chambers were six cubits on this side, and six cubits on that side.

13 - He measured then the gate from the roof of one little chamber to the roof of another: the breadth was five and twenty cubits, door against door.

14 - He made also posts of threescore cubits, even unto the post of the court round about the gate.

15 - And from the face of the gate of the entrance unto the face of the porch of the inner gate were fifty cubits.

EZEKIEL

16. And there were narrow windows to the little chambers, and to their posts within the gate round about, and likewise to the arches: and windows were round about inward: and upon each post were palm trees.

17. Then brought he me into the outward court, and, lo, there were chambers, and a pavement made for the court round about: thirty chambers were upon the pavement.

18. And the pavement by the side of the gates over against the length of the gates was the lower pavement.

19. Then he measured the breadth from the forefront of the lower gate unto the forefront of the inner court without, an hundred cubits eastward and northward.

20. And the gate of the outward court that looked toward the north, he measured the length thereof, and the breadth thereof.

EZEKIEL

2:1 And the little chambers thereof were three on this side and three on that side; and the posts thereof and the arches thereof were after the measure of the first gate: the length thereof was fifty cubits, and the breadth five and twenty cubits.

2:2 And their windows, and their arches, and their palm trees, were after the measure of the gate that looketh toward the east; and they went up unto it by seven steps; and the arches thereof were before them.

2:3 And the gate of the inner court was over against the gate toward the north, and toward the east; and he measured from gate to gate an hundred cubits.

2:4 After that he brought me toward the south, and behold a gate toward the south: and he measured the posts thereof and the arches thereof according to these measures.

EZEKIEL

25- And there were windows in it and in the arches thereof round about, like those windows: the length was fifty cubits, and the breadth five and twenty cubits.

26- And there were seven steps to go up to it, and the arches thereof were before them: and it had palm trees, one on this side, and another on that side, upon the posts thereof.

27- And there was a gate in the inner court toward the south: and he measured from gate to gate toward the south an hundred cubits.

28- And he brought me to the inner court by the south gate: and he measured the south gate according to these measures;

29- And the little chambers thereof, and the posts thereof, and the arches thereof, according to these measures: and there were windows in it and in the arches thereof round about: it was fifty cubits long, and five and twenty cubits broad.

30 - And the arches round about were five and twenty cubits long, and five cubits broad.

31 - And the arches thereof were toward the utter court and palm trees were upon the posts thereof: and the going up to it had eight steps.

32 - And he brought me into the inner court toward the east: and he measured the gate according to these measures.

33 - And the little chambers thereof, and the posts thereof, and the arches thereof, were according to these measures: and there were windows therein and in the arches thereof round about: it was fifty cubits long, and five and twenty cubits broad.

34 - And the arches thereof were toward the outward court: and palm trees were upon the posts thereof, on this side, and on that side: and the going up to it had eight steps.

35 - And he brought me to the north gate, and measured it according to these measures;

EZEKIEL

3:6 The little chambers thereof, the posts thereof, and the arches thereof, and the windows to it round about: the length was fifty cubits, and the breadth five and twenty cubits.

3:7 And the posts thereof were toward the utter court; and palm trees were upon the posts thereof, on this side, and on that side: and the going up to it had eight steps.

3:8 And the chambers and the entries thereof were by the posts of the gates, where they washed the burnt offering.

3:9 And in the porch of the gate were two tables on this side, and two tables on that side, to slay thereon the burnt offering and the sin offering and the trespass offering.

4:0 And at the side without, as one goeth up to the entry of the north gate, were two tables; and on the other side, which was at the porch of the gate, were two tables.

EZEKIEL

41 Four tables were on this side, and four tables on that side, by the side of the gate; eight tables, whereupon they slew their sacrifices.

42 And the four tables were of hewn stone for the burnt offering, of a cubit and an half long, and a cubit and an half broad, and one cubit high: whereupon also they laid the instruments wherewith they slew the burnt offering and the sacrifice.

43 And within were hooks, an hand broad, fastened round about: and upon the tables was the flesh of the offering.

44 And without the inner gate were the chambers of the singers in the inner court, which was at the side of the north gate; and their prospect was toward the south: one at the side of the east gate having the prospect toward the north.

EZEKIEL

45 And he said unto me, This chamber, whose prospect is toward the south, is for the priests, the keepers of the charge of the house.

46 And the chamber whose prospect is toward the north is for the priests, the keepers of the charge of the altar: these are the sons of Zadok among the sons of Levi, which come near to the LORD to minister unto him.

47 So he measured the court, an hundred cubits long, and an hundred cubits broad, foursquare; and the altar that was before the house.

48 And he brought me to the porch of the house, and measured each post of the porch, five cubits on this side, and five cubits on that side: and the breadth of the gate was three cubits on this side, and three cubits on that side.

EZEKIEL

4-9 The length of the porch was twenty cubits, and the breadth eleven cubits; and he brought me by the steps whereby they went up to it: and there were pillars by the posts, one on this side, and another on that side.

CHAPTER 41

1 Afterward he brought me to the temple, and measured the posts, six cubits broad on the one side, and six cubits broad on the other side, which was the breadth of the tabernacle.

2 And the breadth of the door was ten cubits; and the sides of the door were five cubits on the one side, and five cubits on the other side: and he measured the length thereof, forty cubits: and the breadth, twenty cubits.

3 Then went he inward, and measured the post of the door, two cubits; and the door, six cubits; and the breadth of the door, seven cubits.

216

EZEKIEL

4 So he measured the length thereof, twenty cubits; and the breadth, twenty cubits, before the temple: and he said unto me, This is the most holy place.

5 After he measured the wall of the house, six cubits; and the breadth of every side chamber, four cubits, round about the house on every side.

6 And the side chambers were three, one over another, and thirty in order; and they entered into the wall which was of the house for the side chambers round about, that they might have hold, but they had not hold in the wall of the house.

7 And there was an enlarging, and a winding about still upward to the side chambers: for the winding about of the house went still upward round about the house: therefore the breadth of the house was still upward, and so increased from the lowest chamber to the highest by the midst.

EZEKIEL

8 I saw also the height of the house round about: the foundations of the side chambers were a full reed of six great cubits.

9 The thickness of the wall, which was for the side chamber without, was five cubits: and that which was left was the place of the side chambers that were within.

10 And between the chambers was the wideness of twenty cubits round about the house on every side.

11 And the doors of the side chambers were toward the place that was left, one door toward the north, and another door toward the south: and the breadth of the place that was left was five cubits round about.

12 Now the building that was before the separate place at the end toward the west was seventy cubits broad; and the wall of the building was five cubits thick round about, and the length thereof ninety cubits.

EZEKIEL

13 So he measured the house, an hundred cubits long, and the separate place, and the building, with the walls thereof, an hundred cubits long.

14 Also the breadth of the face of the house, and of the separate place toward the east, an hundred cubits.

15 And he measured the length of the building over against the separate place which was behind it, and the galleries thereof on the one side and on the other side, an hundred cubits, with the inner temple, and the porches of the court;

16 The door posts, and the narrow windows, and the galleries round about on their three stories, over against the door, cieled with wood round about, and from the ground up to the windows, and the windows were covered;

17 To that above the door, even unto the inner house, and without, and by all the wall round about within and without, by measure.

EZEKIEL

18 And it was made with cherubims and palm trees, so that a palm tree was between a cherub and a cherub; and every cherub had two faces;

19 So that the face of a man was toward the palm tree on the one side, and the face of a young lion toward the palm tree on the other side: it was made through all the house round about.

20 From the ground unto above the door were cherubims and palm trees made, and on the wall of the temple.

21 The posts of the temple were squared, and the face of the sanctuary; the appearance of the one as the appearance of the other.

22 The altar of wood was three cubits high, and the length thereof two cubits; and the corners thereof, and the length thereof, and the walls thereof, were of wood: and he said unto me, This is the table that is before the LORD.

23 And the temple and the sanctuary had two doors

EZEKIEL

24- And the doors had two leaves apiece, two turning leaves; two leaves for the one door, and two leaves for the other door.

25- And there were made on them, on the doors of the temple, cherubims and palm trees, like as were made upon the walls; and there were thick planks upon the face of the porch without.

26- And there were narrow windows and palm trees on the one side and on the other side, on the sides of the porch, and upon the side chambers of the house, and thick planks.

CHAPTER 42

1- Then he brought me forth into the utter court, the way toward the north: and he brought me into the chamber that was over against the separate place, and which was before the building toward the north.

2- Before the length of an hundred cubits was the north door, and the breadth was fifty cubits.

3 Over against the twenty cubits which were for the inner court, and over against the pavement which was for the utter court, was gallery against gallery in three stories.

4 And before the chambers was a walk of ten cubits breadth inward, a way of one cubit; and their doors toward the north.

5 Now the upper chambers were shorter: for the galleries were higher than these, than the lower, and than the middlemost of the building.

6 For they were in three stories, but had not pillars as the pillars of the courts: therefore the building was straitened more than the lowest and the middlemost from the ground.

7 And the wall that was without over against the chambers, toward the utter court on the forepart of the chambers, the length thereof was fifty cubits.

8 For the length of the chambers that were in the utter court was fifty cubits: and lo, before the temple were an hundred cubits.

EZEKIEL

9 And from under these chambers was the entry on the east side, as one goeth into them from the utter court.

10 The chambers were in the thickness of the wall of the court toward the east, over against the separate place, and over against the building.

11 And the way before them was like the appearance of the chambers which were toward the north, as long as they, and as broad as they: and all their goings out were both according to their fashions, and according to their doors.

12 And according to the doors of the chambers that were toward the south was a door in the head of the way, even the way directly before the wall toward the east, as one entereth into them.

EZEKIEL

13 Then said he unto me, The north chambers and the south chambers, which are before the separate place; they be holy chambers, where the priests that approach unto the LORD shall eat the most holy things: there shall they lay the most holy things, and the meat offering, and the sin offering, and the trespass offering; for the place is holy.

14 When the priests enter therein, then shall they not go out of the holy place into the utter court, but there they shall lay their garments wherein they minister; for they are holy; and shall put on other garments, and shall approach to those things which are for the people.

15 Now when he had made an end of measuring the inner house, he brought me forth toward the gate whose prospect is toward the east, and measured it round about.

16 He measured the east side with the measuring reed, five hundred reeds, with the measuring reed round about.

EZEKIEL

17 He measured the north side, five hundred reeds, with the measuring reed round about.

18 He measured the south side, five hundred reeds, with the measuring reed.

19 He turned about to the west side, and measured five hundred reeds with the measuring reed.

20 He measured it by the four sides: it had a wall round about, five hundred reeds long, and five hundred broad, to make a separation between the sanctuary and the profane place.

CHAPTER 43

1 Afterward he brought me to the gate, even the gate that looketh toward the east:

2 And, behold, the glory of the God of Israel came from the way of the east: and his voice was like a noise of many waters: and the earth shined with his glory.

EZEKIEL

3 And it was according to the appearance of the vision which I saw, even according to the vision that I saw when I came to destroy the city: and the visions were like the vision that I saw by the river Chebar; and I fell upon my face.

4 And the glory of the LORD came into the house by the way of the gate whose prospect is toward the east.

5 So the spirit took me up, and brought me into the inner court; and behold, the glory of the LORD filled the house.

6 And I heard him speaking unto me out of the house; and the man stood by me.

7 And he said unto me, Son of man, the place of my throne, and the place of the soles of my feet, where I will dwell in the midst of the children of Israel for ever, and my holy name, shall the house of Israel no more defile, neither they, nor their kings, by their whoredom, nor by the carcases of their kings in their high places.

EZEKIEL

8 In their setting of their threshold by my thresholds, and their post by my posts, and the wall between me and them, they have even defiled my holy name by their abominations that they have committed: wherefore I have consumed them in mine anger.

9 Now let them put away their whoredom, and the carcases of their kings, far from me, and I will dwell in the midst of them for ever.

10 Thou son of man, shew the house to the house of Israel, that they may be ashamed of their iniquities: and let them measure the pattern.

11 And if they be ashamed of all that they have done, shew them the form of the house, and the fashion thereof, and the goings out thereof, and the comings in thereof, and all the forms thereof, and all the ordinances thereof, and all the forms thereof, and all the laws thereof: and write it in their sight, that they may keep the whole form thereof, and all the ordinances thereof, and do them.

EZEKIEL

12 This is the law of the house: Upon the top of the mountain the whole limit thereof round about shall be most holy. Behold, this is the law of the house.

13 And these are the measures of the altar after the cubits: The cubit is a cubit and an hand breadth; even the bottom shall be a cubit, and the breadth a cubit, and the border thereof by the edge thereof round about shall be a span: and this shall be the higher place of the altar.

14 And from the bottom upon the ground even to the lower settle shall be two cubits, and the breadth one cubit; and from the lesser settle even to the greater settle shall be four cubits, and the breadth one cubit.

15 So the altar shall be four cubits; and from the altar and upward shall be four horns.

16 And the altar shall be twelve cubits long, twelve broad, square in the four squares thereof.

EZEKIEL

17 And the settle shall be fourteen cubits long and fourteen broad in the four squares thereof; and the border about it shall be half a cubit; and the bottom thereof shall be a cubit about; and his stairs shall look toward the east.

18 And he said unto me, Son of man, thus saith the Lord GOD; These are the ordinances of the altar in the day when they shall make it, to offer burnt offerings thereon, and to sprinkle blood thereon.

19 And thou shalt give to the priests the Levites that be of the seed of Zadok, which approach unto me, to minister unto me, saith the Lord GOD, a young bullock for a sin offering.

20 And thou shalt take of the blood thereof, and put it on the four horns of it, and on the four corners of the settle, and upon the border round about: thus shalt thou cleanse and purge it.

EZEKIEL

24 Thou shalt take the bullock also of the sin offering, and he shall burn it in the appointed place of the house, without the sanctuary.

2 2 And on the second day thou shalt offer a kid of the goats without blemish for a sin offering; and they shall cleanse the altar, as they did cleanse it with the bullock.

2 3 When thou hast made an end of cleansing it, thou shalt offer a young bullock without blemish, and a ram out of the flock without blemish.

2 4 And thou shalt offer them before the LORD, and the priests shall cast salt upon them, and they shall offer them up for a burnt offering unto the LORD.

2 5 Seven days shalt thou prepare every day a goat for a sin offering: they shall also prepare a young bullock, and a ram out of the flock, without blemish.

2 6 Seven days shall they purge the altar and purify it; and they shall consecrate themselves.

EZEKIEL

27 And when these days are expired, it shall be, that upon the eighth day, and so forward, the priests shall make your burnt offerings upon the altar, and your peace offerings; and I will accept you, saith the Lord GOD.

CHAPTER 44

1 Then he brought me back the way of the gate of the outward sanctuary which looketh toward the east; and it was shut.

2 Then said the LORD unto me; This gate shall be shut, it shall not be opened, and no man shall enter in by it; because the LORD, the God of Israel, hath entered in by it, therefore it shall be shut.

3 It is for the prince; the prince, he shall sit in it to eat bread before the LORD; he shall enter by the way of the porch of that gate, and shall go out by the way of the same.

4 Then brought he me the way of the north gate before the house: and I looked, and behold, the glory of the LORD filled the house of the LORD: and I fell upon my face.

5 And the LORD said unto me, Son of man, mark well, and behold with thine eyes, and hear with thine ears all that I say unto thee concerning all the ordinances of the house of the LORD, and all the laws thereof; and mark well the entering in of the house, with every going forth of the sanctuary.

6 And thou shalt say to the rebellious, even to the house of Israel, Thus saith the Lord GOD; O ye house of Israel, let it suffice you of all your abominations,

7 In that ye have brought into my sanctuary strangers, uncircumcised in heart, and uncircumcised in flesh, to be in my sanctuary, to pollute it, even my house, when ye offer my bread, the fat and the blood, and they have broken my covenant because of all your abominations.

EZEKIEL

8 - And ye have not kept the charge of mine holy things: but ye have set keepers of my charge in my sanctuary for yourselves.

9 - Thus saith the Lord GOD; No stranger, uncircumcised in heart, nor uncircumcised in flesh, shall enter into my sanctuary, of any stranger that is among the children of Israel.

10 - And the Levites that are gone away far from me, when Israel went astray, which went astray away from me after their idols; they shall even bear their iniquity.

11 - Yet they shall be ministers in my sanctuary, having charge at the gates of the house, and ministering to the house: they shall slay the burnt offering and the sacrifice for the people, and they shall stand before them to minister unto them.

EZEKIEL

12 Because they ministered unto them before their idols, and caused the house of Israel to fall into iniquity; therefore have I lifted up mine hand against them, saith the Lord GOD, and they shall bear their iniquity.

13 And they shall not come near unto me, to do the office of a priest unto me, nor to come near to any of my holy things, in the most holy place: but they shall bear their shame, and their abominations which they have committed.

14 But I will make them keepers of the charge of the house, for all the service thereof, and for all that shall be done therein.

15 But the priests the Levites, the sons of Zadok, that kept the charge of my sanctuary when the children of Israel went astray from me, they shall come near to me to minister unto me, and they shall stand before me to offer unto me the fat and the blood, saith the Lord GOD:

EZEKIEL

16 They shall enter into my sanctuary, and they shall come near to my table, to minister unto me, and they shall keep my charge.

17 And it shall come to pass, that when they enter in at the gates of the inner court, they shall be clothed with linen garments; and no wool shall come upon them, whiles they minister in the gates of the inner court, and within.

18 They shall have linen bonnets upon their heads, and shall have linen breeches upon their loins; they shall not gird themselves with any thing that causeth sweat.

19 And when they go forth into the utter court, even into the utter court to the people, they shall put off their garments wherein they ministered, and lay them in the holy chambers, and they shall put on other garments; and they shall not sanctify the people with their garments.

EZEKIEL

20 Neither shall they shave their heads, nor suffer their locks to grow long; they shall only poll their heads.

21 Neither shall any priest drink wine, when they enter into the inner court.

22 Neither shall they take for their wives a widow, nor her that is put away: but they shall take maidens of the seed of the house of Israel, or a widow that had a priest before.

23 And they shall teach my people the difference between the holy and profane, and cause them to discern between the unclean and the clean.

24 And in controversy they shall stand in judgment; and they shall judge it according to my judgments: and they shall keep my laws and my statutes in all mine assemblies; and they shall hallow my sabbaths.

25 And they shall come at no dead person to defile themselves: but for father, or for mother, or for son, or for daughter, for brother, or for sister that hath had no husband, they may defile themselves.

EZEKIEL

26 And after he is cleansed, they shall reckon unto
him seven days.

27 And in the day that he goeth into the sanctuary,
unto the inner court, to minister in the sanctuary, he
shall offer his sin offering, saith the Lord GOD.

28 And it shall be unto them for an inheritance: I am
their inheritance: and ye shall give them no possession
in Israel: I am their possession.

29 They shall eat the meat offering, and the sin
offering, and the trespass offering; and every
dedicated thing in Israel shall be theirs.

30 And the first of all the firstfruits of all things,
and every oblation of all, of every sort of your
oblations, shall be the priest's: ye shall also give unto
the priest the first of your dough, that he may cause
the blessing to rest in thine house.

31 The priests shall not eat of any thing that is dead
of itself, or torn, whether it be fowl or beast.

EZEKIEL

CHAPTER 45

1 Moreover, when ye shall divide by lot the land for inheritance, ye shall offer an oblation unto the LORD, an holy portion of the land: the length shall be the length of five and twenty thousand reeds, and the breadth shall be ten thousand. This shall be holy in all the borders thereof round about.

2 Of this there shall be for the sanctuary five hundred in length, with five hundred in breadth, square round about; and fifty cubits round about for the suburbs thereof.

3 And of this measure shalt thou measure the length of five and twenty thousand, and the breadth of ten thousand: and in it shall be the sanctuary and the most holy place.

4 The holy portion of the land shall be for the priests the ministers of the sanctuary, which shall come near to minister unto the LORD: and it shall be a place for their houses, and an holy place for the sanctuary.

EZEKIEL

5 And the five and twenty thousand of length, and the ten thousand of breadth, shall also the Levites, the ministers of the house, have for themselves, for a possession for twenty chambers.

6 And ye shall appoint the possession of the city five thousand broad, and five and twenty thousand long, over against the oblation of the holy portion: it shall be for the whole house of Israel.

7 And a portion shall be for the prince on the one side and on the other side of the oblation of the holy portion, and of the possession of the city, before the oblation of the holy portion, and before the possession of the city, from the west side westward, and from the east side eastward: and the length shall be over against one of the portions, from the west border unto the east border.

EZEKIEL

8 In the land shall be his possession in Israel: and my princes shall no more oppress my people; and the rest of the land shall they give to the house of Israel according to their tribes.

9 Thus saith the Lord GOD; Let it suffice you, O princes of Israel: remove violence and spoil, and execute judgment and justice, take away your exactions from my people, saith the Lord GOD.

10 Ye shall have just balances, and a just ephah, and a just bath.

11 The ephah and the bath shall be of one measure, that the bath may contain the tenth part of an homer, and the ephah the tenth part of an homer: the measure thereof shall be after the homer.

12 And the shekel shall be twenty gerahs: twenty shekels, five and twenty shekels, fifteen shekels, shall be your maneh.

EZEKIEL

13 This is the oblation that ye shall offer; the sixth part of an ephah of an homer of wheat, and ye shall give the sixth part of an ephah of an homer of barley:

14 Concerning the ordinance of oil, the bath of oil, ye shall offer the tenth part of a bath out of the cor, which is an homer of ten baths; for ten baths are an homer:

15 And one lamb out of the flock, out of two hundred, out of the fat pastures of Israel; for a meat offering, and for a burnt offering, and for peace offerings, to make reconciliation for them, saith the Lord GOD.

16 All the people of the land shall give this oblation for the prince in Israel.

17 And it shall be the prince's part to give burnt offerings, and meat offerings, and drink offerings, in the feasts, and in the new moons, and in the sabbaths, in all solemnities of the house of Israel: he shall prepare the sin offering, and the meat offering, and the burnt offering, and the peace offerings, to make reconciliation for the house of Israel.

EZEKIEL

18 Thus saith the Lord GOD; In the first month, in the first day of the month, thou shalt take a young bullock without blemish, and cleanse the sanctuary:

19 And the priest shall take of the blood of the sin offering, and put it upon the posts of the house, and upon the four corners of the settle of the altar, and upon the posts of the gate of the inner court.

20 And so thou shalt do the seventh day of the month for every one that erreth, and for him that is simple: so shall ye reconcile the house.

21 In the first month, in the fourteenth day of the month, ye shall have the passover, a feast of seven days; unleavened bread shall be eaten.

22 And upon that day shall the prince prepare for himself and for all the people of the land a bullock for a sin offering.

EZEKIEL

23 And seven days of the feast he shall prepare a burnt offering to the LORD, seven bullocks and seven rams without blemish daily the seven days, and a kid of the goats daily for a sin offering.

24 And he shall prepare a meat offering of an ephah for a bullock, and an ephah for a ram, and an hin of oil for an ephah.

25 In the seventh month, in the fifteenth day of the month, shall he do the like in the feast of the seven days, according to the sin offering, according to the burnt offering, and according to the meat offering, and according to the oil.

CHAPTER 46

1 Thus saith the Lord GOD; The gate of the inner court that looketh toward the east shall be shut the six working days; but on the sabbath it shall be opened, and in the day of the new moon it shall be opened.

EZEKIEL

2 And the prince shall enter by the way of the porch of that gate without, and shall stand by the post of the gate, and the priests shall prepare his burnt offering and his peace offerings, and he shall worship at the threshold of the gate: then he shall go forth; but the gate shall not be shut until the evening.

3 Likewise the people of the land shall worship at the door of this gate before the LORD in the sabbaths and in the new moons.

4 And the burnt offering that the prince shall offer unto the LORD in the sabbath day shall be six lambs without blemish, and a ram without blemish.

5 And the meat offering shall be an ephah for a ram, and the meat offering for the lambs as he shall be able to give, and an hin of oil to an ephah.

6 And in the day of the new moon it shall be a young bullock without blemish, and six lambs, and a ram: they shall be without blemish.

EZEKIEL

7 And he shall prepare a meat offering, an ephah for a bullock, and an ephah for a ram, and for the lambs according as his hand shall attain unto, and an hin of oil to an ephah.

8 And when the prince shall enter, he shall go in by the way of the porch of that gate, and he shall go forth by the way thereof.

9 But when the people of the land shall come before the LORD in the solemn feasts, he that entereth in by the way of the north gate to worship shall go out by the way of the south gate; and he that entereth by the way of the south gate shall go forth by the way of the north gate: he shall not return by the way of the gate whereby he came in, but shall go forth over against it.

10 And the prince in the midst of them, when they go in, shall go in; and when they go forth, shall go forth.

EZEKIEL

11 And in the feasts and in the solemnities the meat offering shall be an ephah to a bullock, and an ephah to a ram, and to the lambs as he is able to give, and an hin of oil to an ephah.

12 Now when the prince shall prepare a voluntary burnt offering or peace offerings voluntarily unto the LORD, one shall then open him the gate that looketh toward the east, and he shall prepare his burnt offering and his peace offerings, as he did on the sabbath day: then he shall go forth; and after his going forth one shall shut the gate.

13 Thou shalt daily prepare a burnt offering unto the LORD of a lamb of the first year without blemish: thou shalt prepare it every morning.

14 And thou shalt prepare a meat offering for it every morning, the sixth part of an ephah, and the third part of an hin of oil, to temper with the fine flour; a meat offering continually by a perpetual ordinance unto the LORD.

EZEKIEL

15 Thus shall they prepare the lamb, and the meat offering, and the oil, every morning for a continual burnt offering.

16 Thus saith the Lord GOD; If the prince give a gift unto any of his sons, the inheritance thereof shall be his sons; it shall be their possession by inheritance.

17 But if he give a gift of his inheritance to one of his servants, then it shall be his to the year of liberty; after it shall return to the prince: but his inheritance shall be his sons for them.

18 Moreover the prince shall not take of the people's inheritance by oppression, to thrust them out of their possession; but he shall give his sons inheritance out of his own possession: that my people be not scattered every man from his possession.

19 After he brought me through the entry, which was at the side of the gate, into the holy chambers of the priests, which looked toward the north: and, behold, there was a place on the two sides westward.

EZEKIEL

20 Then said he unto me, This is the place where the priests shall boil the trespass offering and the sin offering, where they shall bake the meat offering; that they bear them not out into the utter court, to sanctify the people.

21 Then he brought me forth into the utter court, and caused me to pass by the four corners of the court; and, behold, in every corner of the court there was a court.

22 In the four corners of the court there were courts joined of forty cubits long and thirty broad: these four corners were of one measure.

23 And there was a row of building round about in them, round about them four, and it was made with boiling places under the rows round about.

24 Then said he unto me, These are the places of them that boil, where the ministers of the house shall boil the sacrifice of the people.

EZEKIEL

CHAPTER 47

1 Afterward he brought me again unto the door of the house; and, behold, waters issued out from under the threshold of the house eastward: for the forefront of the house stood toward the east, and the waters came down from under from the right side of the house, at the south side of the altar.

2 Then brought he me out of the way of the gate northward, and led me about the way without unto the utter gate by the way that looketh eastward; and, behold, there ran out waters on the right side.

3 And when the man that had the line in his hand went forth eastward, he measured a thousand cubits, and he brought me through the waters; the waters were to the ankles.

4 Again he measured a thousand, and brought me through the waters; the waters were to the knees. Again he measured a thousand, and brought me through; the waters were to the loins.

5 Afterward he measured a thousand; and it was a river that I could not pass over: for the waters were risen, waters to swim in, a river that could not be passed over.

6 And he said unto me, Son of man, hast thou seen this? Then he brought me, and caused me to return to the brink of the river.

7 Now when I had returned, behold, at the bank of the river were very many trees on the one side and on the other.

8 Then said he unto me, These waters issue out toward the east country, and go down into the desert, and go into the sea: which being brought forth into the sea, the waters shall be healed.

9 And it shall come to pass, that every thing that liveth, which moveth, whithersoever the rivers shall come, shall live: and there shall be a very great multitude of fish, because these waters shall come thither: for they shall be healed; and every thing shall live whither the river cometh.

EZEKIEL

10 - And it shall come to pass, that the fishers shall stand upon it from En-gedi even unto En-eglaim; they shall be a place to spread forth nets; their fish shall be according to their kinds, as the fish of the great sea, exceeding many.

11 But the miry places thereof and the marishes thereof shall not be healed; they shall be given to salt.

12 - And by the river upon the bank thereof, on this side and on that side, shall grow all trees for meat, whose leaf shall not fade, neither shall the fruit thereof be consumed: it shall bring forth new fruit according to his months, because their waters they issued out of the sanctuary: and the fruit thereof shall be for meat, and the leaf thereof for medicine.

13 - Thus saith the Lord GOD; This shall be the border, whereby ye shall inherit the land according to the twelve tribes of Israel: Joseph shall have two portions.

EZEKIEL

14. And ye shall inherit it, one as well as another: concerning the which I lifted up mine hand to give it unto your fathers: and this land shall fall unto you for inheritance.

15. And this shall be the border of the land toward the north side, from the great sea, the way of Hethlon, as men go to Zedad;

16. Hamath, Berothah, Sibraim, which is between the border of Damascus and the border of Hamath; Hazar-hatticon, which is by the coast of Hauran.

17. And the border from the sea shall be Hazar-enan, the border of Damascus, and the north northward, and the border of Hamath. And this is the north side.

18. And the east side ye shall measure from Hauran, and from Damascus, and from Gilead, and from the land of Israel by Jordan, from the border unto the east sea. And this is the east side.

EZEKIEL

19 And the south side southward, from Tamar even to the waters of strife in Kadesh, the river to the great sea. And this is the south side southward.

20 The west side also shall be the great sea from the border, till a man come over against Hamath. This is the west side.

21 So shall ye divide this land unto you according to the tribes of Israel.

22 And it shall come to pass, that ye shall divide it by lot for an inheritance unto you, and to the strangers that sojourn among you, which shall beget children among you: and they shall be unto you as born in the country among the children of Israel; they shall have inheritance with you among the tribes of Israel.

23 And it shall come to pass, that in what tribe the stranger sojourneth, there shall ye give him his inheritance, saith the Lord GOD.

CHAPTER 48

1 Now these are the names of the tribes. From the north end to the coast of the way of Hethlon, as one goeth to Hamath, Hazar-enan, the border of Damascus northward, to the coast of Hamath; for these are his sides east and west; a portion for Dan.

2 And by the border of Dan, from the east side unto the west side, a portion for Asher.

3 And by the border of Asher, from the east side even unto the west side, a portion for Naphtali.

4 And by the border of Naphtali, from the east side unto the west side, a portion for Manasseh.

5 And by the border of Manasseh, from the east side unto the west side, a portion for Ephraim.

6 And by the border of Ephraim, from the east side even unto the west side, a portion for Reuben.

EZEKIEL

7 And by the border of Reuben, from the east side unto the west side, a portion for Judah.

8 And by the border of Judah, from the east side unto the west side, shall be the offering which ye shall offer of five and twenty thousand reeds in breadth, and in length as one of the other parts, from the east side unto the west side: and the sanctuary shall be in the midst of it.

9 The oblation that ye shall offer unto the LORD shall be of five and twenty thousand in length, and of ten thousand in breadth.

10 And for them, even for the priests, shall be this holy oblation; toward the north five and twenty thousand in length, and toward the west ten thousand in breadth, and toward the east ten thousand in breadth, and toward the south five and twenty thousand in length: and the sanctuary of the LORD shall be in the midst thereof.

EZEKIEL

1 It shall be for the priests that are sanctified of the sons of Zadok; which have kept my charge, which went not astray when the children of Israel went astray, as the Levites went astray.

2 And this oblation of the land that is offered shall be unto them a thing most holy by the border of the Levites.

3 And over against the border of the priests the Levites shall have five and twenty thousand in length, and ten thousand in breadth: all the length shall be five and twenty thousand, and the breadth ten thousand.

4 And they shall not sell of it, neither exchange, nor alienate the firstfruits of the land: for it is holy unto the LORD.

5 And the five thousand, that are left in the breadth over against the five and twenty thousand, shall be a profane place for the city, for dwelling, and for suburbs: and the city shall be in the midst thereof.

EZEKIEL

16 And these shall be the measures thereof; the north side four thousand and five hundred, and the south side four thousand and five hundred, and on the east side four thousand and five hundred, and the west side four thousand and five hundred.

17 And the suburbs of the city shall be toward the north two hundred and fifty, and toward the south two hundred and fifty, and toward the east two hundred and fifty, and toward the west two hundred and fifty.

18 And the residue in length over against the oblation of the holy portion shall be ten thousand eastward, and ten thousand westward: and it shall be over against the oblation of the holy portion; and the increase thereof shall be for food unto them that serve the city.

19 And they that serve the city shall serve it out of all the tribes of Israel.

EZEKIEL

20 All the oblation shall be five and twenty thousand by five and twenty thousand: ye shall offer the holy oblation foursquare, with the possession of the city.

21 And the residue shall be for the prince, on the one side and on the other of the holy oblation, and of the possession of the city, over against the five and twenty thousand of the oblation toward the east border, and westward over against the five and twenty thousand toward the west border, over against the portions for the prince: and it shall be the holy oblation; and the sanctuary of the house shall be in the midst thereof.

22 Moreover from the possession of the Levites, and from the possession of the city, being in the midst of that which is the prince's, between the border of Judah and the border of Benjamin, shall be for the prince.

EZEKIEL

23. As for the rest of the tribes, from the east side unto the west side, Benjamin shall have a portion.

24. And by the border of Benjamin, from the east side unto the west side, Simeon shall have a portion.

25. And by the border of Simeon, from the east side unto the west side, Issachar a portion.

26. And by the border of Issachar, from the east side unto the west side, Zebulun a portion.

27. And by the border of Zebulun, from the east side unto the west side, Gad a portion.

28. And by the border of Gad, at the south side southward, the border shall be even from Tamar unto the waters of strife in Kadesh, and to the river toward the great sea.

29. This is the land which ye shall divide by lot unto the tribes of Israel for inheritance, and these are their portions, saith the Lord GOD.

EZEKIEL

30 And these are the goings out of the city on the north side, four thousand and five hundred measures.

31 And the gates of the city shall be after the names of the tribes of Israel: three gates northward; one gate of Reuben, one gate of Judah, one gate of Levi.

32 And at the east side four thousand and five hundred: and three gates; and one gate of Joseph, one gate of Benjamin, one gate of Dan.

33 And at the south side four thousand and five hundred measures: and three gates; one gate of Simeon, one gate of Issachar, one gate of Zebulun.

34 At the west side four thousand and five hundred, with their three gates; one gate of Gad, one gate of Asher, one gate of Naphtali.

35 It was round about eighteen thousand measures: and the name of the city from that day shall be, The LORD is there.

THE BOOK OF
DANIEL

DANIEL

CHAPTER 1

1 In the third year of the reign of Jehoiakim king of Judah came Nebuchadnezzar king of Babylon unto Jerusalem, and besieged it.

2 And the Lord gave Jehoiakim king of Judah into his hand, with part of the vessels of the house of God: which he carried into the land of Shinar to the house of his god; and he brought the vessels into the treasure house of his god.

3 And the king spake unto Ashpenaz the master of his eunuchs, that he should bring certain of the children of Israel, and of the king's seed, and of the princes;

4 Children in whom was no blemish, but well favoured, and skilful in all wisdom, and cunning in knowledge, and understanding science, and such as had ability in them to stand in the king's palace, and whom they might teach the learning and the tongue of the Chaldeans.

DANIEL

5 And the king appointed them a daily provision of
the king's meat, and of the wine which he drank: so
nourishing them three years, that at the end thereof
they might stand before the king.
6 Now among these were of the children of Judah,
Daniel, Hananiah, Mishael, and Azariah:
7 Unto whom the prince of the eunuchs gave names:
for he gave unto Daniel the name of Belteshazzar;
and to Hananiah, of Shadrach; and to Mishael, of
Meshach; and to Azariah, of Abed-nego.
8 But Daniel purposed in his heart that he would not
defile himself with the portion of the king's meat, nor
with the wine which he drank: therefore he requested
of the prince of the eunuchs that he might not defile
himself.
9 Now God had brought Daniel into favour and
tender love with the prince of the eunuchs.

DANIEL

And the prince of the eunuchs said unto Daniel, I fear my lord the king, who hath appointed your meat and your drink: for why should he see your faces worse liking than the children which are of your sort? then shall ye make me endanger my head to the king.

11 Then said Daniel to Melzar, whom the prince of the eunuchs had set over Daniel, Hananiah, Mishael, and Azariah,

12 Prove thy servants, I beseech thee, ten days; and let them give us pulse to eat, and water to drink.

13 Then let our countenances be looked upon before thee, and the countenance of the children that eat of the portion of the king's meat: and as thou seest, deal with thy servants.

14 So he consented to them in this matter, and proved them ten days.

15 And at the end of ten days their countenances appeared fairer and fatter in flesh than all the children which did eat the portion of the king's meat.

DANIEL

16 Thus Melzar took away the portion of their meat, and the wine that they should drink, and gave them pulse.

17 As for these four children, God gave them knowledge and skill in all learning and wisdom: and Daniel had understanding in all visions and dreams.

18 Now at the end of the days that the king had said he should bring them in, then the prince of the eunuchs brought them in before Nebuchadnezzar.

19 And the king communed with them; and among them all was found none like Daniel, Hananiah, Mishael, and Azariah: therefore stood they before the king.

20 And in all matters of wisdom and understanding, that the king enquired of them, he found them ten times better than all the magicians and astrologers that were in all his realm.

21 And Daniel continued even unto the first year of king Cyrus.

DANIEL

CHAPTER 2

1 And in the second year of the reign of Nebuchadnezzar Nebuchadnezzar dreamed dreams, wherewith his spirit was troubled, and his sleep brake from him.

2 Then the king commanded to call the magicians, and the astrologers, and the sorcerers, and the Chaldeans, for to shew the king his dreams. So they came and stood before the king.

3 And the king said unto them, I have dreamed a dream, and my spirit was troubled to know the dream.

4 Then spake the Chaldeans to the king in Syriack, O king, live for ever: tell thy servants the dream, and we will shew the interpretation.

5 The king answered and said to the Chaldeans, The thing is gone from me: if ye will not make known unto me the dream, with the interpretation thereof, ye shall be cut in pieces, and your houses shall be made a dunghill.

DANIEL

6 But if ye shew the dream, and the interpretation thereof, ye shall receive of me gifts and rewards and great honour: therefore shew me the dream, and the interpretation thereof.

7 They answered again and said, Let the king tell his servants the dream, and we will shew the interpretation of it.

8 The king answered and said, I know of certainty that ye would gain the time, because ye see the thing is gone from me.

9 But if ye will not make known unto me the dream, there is but one decree for you: for ye have prepared lying and corrupt words to speak before me, till the time be changed: therefore tell me the dream, and I shall know that ye can shew me the interpretation thereof.

10 The Chaldeans answered before the king, and said, There is not a man upon the earth that can shew the king's matter: therefore there is no king, lord, nor ruler, that asked such things at any magician, or astrologer, or Chaldean.

DANIEL

11 And it is a rare thing that the king requireth, and there is none other that can shew it before the king, except the gods, whose dwelling is not with flesh.

12 For this cause the king was angry and very furious, and commanded to destroy all the wise men of Babylon.

13 And the decree went forth that the wise men should be slain; and they sought Daniel and his fellows to be slain.

14 Then Daniel answered with counsel and wisdom to Arioch the captain of the king's guard, which was gone forth to slay the wise men of Babylon:

15 He answered and said to Arioch the king's captain, Why is the decree so hasty from the king? Then Arioch made the thing known to Daniel.

16 Then Daniel went in, and desired of the king that he would give him time, and that he would shew the king the interpretation.

17 Then Daniel went to his house, and made the thing known to Hananiah, Mishael, and Azariah, his companions:

DANIEL

18 That they would desire mercies of the God of heaven concerning this secret; that Daniel and his fellows should not perish with the rest of the wise men of Babylon.

19 Then was the secret revealed unto Daniel in a night vision. Then Daniel blessed the God of heaven.

20 Daniel answered and said, Blessed be the name of God for ever and ever: for wisdom and might are his:

21 And he changeth the times and the seasons: he removeth kings, and setteth up kings: he giveth wisdom unto the wise, and knowledge to them that know understanding:

22 He revealeth the deep and secret things: he knoweth what is in the darkness, and the light dwelleth with him.

23 I thank thee, and praise thee, O thou God of my fathers, who hast given me wisdom and might, and hast made known unto me now what we desired of thee: for thou hast now made known unto us the king's matter.

DANIEL

2:4 Therefore Daniel went in unto Arioch, whom the king had ordained to destroy the wise men of Babylon: he went and said thus unto him; Destroy not the wise men of Babylon: bring me in before the king, and I will shew unto the king the interpretation.

2:5 Then Arioch brought in Daniel before the king in haste, and said thus unto him, I have found a man of the captives of Judah, that will make known unto the king the interpretation.

2:6 The king answered and said to Daniel, whose name was Belteshazzar, Art thou able to make known unto me the dream which I have seen, and the interpretation thereof?

2:7 Daniel answered in the presence of the king, and said, The secret which the king hath demanded cannot the wise men, the astrologers, the magicians, the soothsayers, shew unto the king;

2-8 But there is a God in heaven that revealeth secrets, and maketh known to the king Nebuchadnezzar what shall be in the latter days. Thy dream, and the visions of thy head upon thy bed, are these;

2-9 As for thee, O king, thy thoughts came into thy mind upon thy bed, what should come to pass hereafter: and he that revealeth secrets maketh known to thee what shall come to pass.

3-0 But as for me, this secret is not revealed to me for any wisdom that I have more than any living, but for their sakes that shall make known the interpretation to the king, and that thou mightest know the thoughts of thy heart.

3-1 Thou, O king, sawest, and behold a great image. This great image, whose brightness was excellent, stood before thee; and the form thereof was terrible.

3-2 This image's head was of fine gold, his breast and his arms of silver, his belly and his thighs of brass,

3-3 His legs of iron, his feet part of iron and part of clay.

DANIEL

34 Thou sawest till that a stone was cut out without hands, which smote the image upon his feet that were of iron and clay, and brake them to pieces.

35 Then was the iron, the clay, the brass, the silver, and the gold, broken to pieces together, and became like the chaff of the summer threshingfloors; and the wind carried them away, that no place was found for them: and the stone that smote the image became a great mountain, and filled the whole earth.

36 This is the dream; and we will tell the interpretation thereof before the king.

37 Thou, O king, art a king of kings: for the God of heaven hath given thee a kingdom, power, and strength, and glory.

38 And wheresoever the children of men dwell, the beasts of the field and the fowls of the heaven hath he given into thine hand, and hath made thee ruler over them all. Thou art this head of gold.

39 And after thee shall arise another kingdom inferior to thee, and another third kingdom of brass, which shall bear rule over all the earth.

DANIEL

40 And the fourth kingdom shall be strong as iron: forasmuch as iron breaketh in pieces and subdueth all things: and as iron that breaketh all these, shall it break in pieces and bruise.

41 And whereas thou sawest the feet and toes, part of potters' clay, and part of iron, the kingdom shall be divided; but there shall be in it of the strength of the iron, forasmuch as thou sawest the iron mixed with miry clay.

42 And as the toes of the feet were part of iron, and part of clay, so the kingdom shall be partly strong, and partly broken.

43 And whereas thou sawest iron mixed with miry clay, they shall mingle themselves with the seed of men: but they shall not cleave one to another, even as iron is not mixed with clay.

44 And in the days of these kings shall the God of heaven set up a kingdom, which shall never be destroyed: and the kingdom shall not be left to other people, but it shall break in pieces and consume all these kingdoms, and it shall stand for ever.

DANIEL

45 Forasmuch as thou sawest that the stone was cut out of the mountain without hands, and that it brake in pieces the iron, the brass, the clay, the silver, and the gold; the great God hath made known to the king what shall come to pass hereafter: and the dream is certain, and the interpretation thereof sure.

46 Then the king Nebuchadnezzar fell upon his face, and worshipped Daniel, and commanded that they should offer an oblation and sweet odours unto him.

47 The king answered unto Daniel, and said, Of a truth it is, that your God is a God of gods, and a Lord of kings, and a revealer of secrets, seeing thou couldest reveal this secret.

48 Then the king made Daniel a great man, and gave him many great gifts, and made him ruler over the whole province of Babylon, and chief of the governors over all the wise men of Babylon.

DANIEL

49 Then Daniel requested of the king, and he set Shadrach, Meshach, and Abed-nego, over the affairs of the province of Babylon: but Daniel sat in the gate of the king.

CHAPTER 3

1 Nebuchadnezzar the king made an image of gold, whose height was threescore cubits, and the breadth thereof six cubits: he set it up in the plain of Dura, in the province of Babylon.

2 Then Nebuchadnezzar the king sent to gather together the princes, the governors, and the captains, the judges, the treasurers, the counsellors, the sheriffs, and all the rulers of the provinces, to come to the dedication of the image which Nebuchadnezzar the king had set up.

DANIEL

3 Then the princes, the governors, and captains, the judges, the treasurers, the counsellors, the sheriffs, and all the rulers of the provinces, were gathered together unto the dedication of the image that Nebuchadnezzar the king had set up; and they stood before the image that Nebuchadnezzar had set up.

4 Then an herald cried aloud, To you it is commanded, O people, nations, and languages,

5 That at what time ye hear the sound of the cornet, flute, harp, sackbut, psaltery, dulcimer, and all kinds of musick, ye fall down and worship the golden image that Nebuchadnezzar the king hath set up:

6 And whoso falleth not down and worshippeth shall the same hour be cast into the midst of a burning fiery furnace.

7 Therefore at that time, when all the people heard the sound of the cornet, flute, harp, sackbut, psaltery, and all kinds of musick, all the people, the nations, and the languages, fell down and worshipped the golden image that Nebuchadnezzar the king had set up.

DANIEL

8 - Wherefore at that time certain Chaldeans came near, and accused the Jews.

9 - They spake and said to the king Nebuchadnezzar, O king, live for ever.

10 - Thou, O king, hast made a decree, that every man that shall hear the sound of the cornet, flute, harp, sackbut, psaltery, and dulcimer, and all kinds of musick, shall fall down and worship the golden image:

11 - And whoso falleth not down and worshippeth, that he should be cast into the midst of a burning fiery furnace.

12 - There are certain Jews whom thou hast set over the affairs of the province of Babylon, Shadrach, Meshach, and Abed-nego; these men, O king, have not regarded thee: they serve not thy gods, nor worship the golden image which thou hast set up.

13 - Then Nebuchadnezzar in his rage and fury commanded to bring Shadrach, Meshach, and Abed-nego. Then they brought these men before the king.

DANIEL

14- Nebuchadnezzar spake and said unto them, Is it true, O Shadrach, Meshach, and Abed-nego, do not ye serve my gods, nor worship the golden image which I have set up?

15- Now if ye be ready that at what time ye hear the sound of the cornet, flute, harp, sackbut, psaltery, and dulcimer, and all kinds of musick, ye fall down and worship the image which I have made; well: but if ye worship not, ye shall be cast the same hour into the midst of a burning fiery furnace; and who is that God that shall deliver you out of my hands?

16- Shadrach, Meshach, and Abed-nego, answered and said to the king, O Nebuchadnezzar, we are not careful to answer thee in this matter.

17- If it be so, our God whom we serve is able to deliver us from the burning fiery furnace, and he will deliver us out of thine hand, O king.

18- But if not, be it known unto thee, O king, that we will not serve thy gods, nor worship the golden image which thou hast set up.

DANIEL

19 Then was Nebuchadnezzar full of fury, and the form of his visage was changed against Shadrach, Meshach, and Abed-nego: therefore he spake, and commanded that they should heat the furnace one seven times more than it was wont to be heated.

20 And he commanded the most mighty men that were in his army to bind Shadrach, Meshach, and Abed-nego, and to cast them into the burning fiery furnace.

21 Then these men were bound in their coats, their hosen, and their hats, and their other garments, and were cast into the midst of the burning fiery furnace.

22 Therefore because the king's commandment was urgent, and the furnace exceeding hot, the flame of the fire slew those men that took up Shadrach, Meshach, and Abed-nego.

23 And these three men, Shadrach, Meshach, and Abed-nego, fell down bound into the midst of the burning fiery furnace.

DANIEL

24 Then Nebuchadnezzar the king was astonied, and rose up in haste, and spake, and said unto his counsellors, Did not we cast three men bound into the midst of the fire? They answered and said unto the king, True, O king.

25 He answered and said, Lo, I see four men loose, walking in the midst of the fire, and they have no hurt; and the form of the fourth is like the Son of God.

26 Then Nebuchadnezzar came near to the mouth of the burning fiery furnace, and spake, and said, Shadrach, Meshach, and Abed-nego, ye servants of the most high God, come forth, and come hither. Then Shadrach, Meshach, and Abed-nego, came forth of the midst of the fire.

27 And the princes, governors, and captains, and the king's counsellors, being gathered together, saw these men, upon whose bodies the fire had no power, nor was an hair of their head singed, neither were their coats changed, nor the smell of fire had passed on them.

DANIEL

2-8 Then Nebuchadnezzar spake, and said, Blessed be the God of Shadrach, Meshach, and Abed-nego, who hath sent his angel, and delivered his servants that trusted in him, and have changed the kings word, and yielded their bodies, that they might not serve nor worship any god, except their own God.

2-9 Therefore I make a decree, That every people, nation, and language, which speak any thing amiss against the God of Shadrach, Meshach, and Abed-nego, shall be cut in pieces, and their houses shall be made a dunghill: because there is no other God that can deliver after this sort.

3-0 Then the king promoted Shadrach, Meshach, and Abed-nego in the province of Babylon.

CHAPTER 4

1 Nebuchadnezzar the king, unto all people, nations, and languages, that dwell in all the earth; Peace be multiplied unto you.

DANIEL

2 I thought it good to shew the signs and wonders that the high God hath wrought toward me.

3 How great are his signs! and how mighty are his wonders! his kingdom is an everlasting kingdom, and his dominion is from generation to generation.

4 I Nebuchadnezzar was at rest in mine house, and flourishing in my palace:

5 I saw a dream which made me afraid, and the thoughts upon my bed and the visions of my head troubled me.

6 Therefore made I a decree to bring in all the wise men of Babylon before me, that they might make known unto me the interpretation of the dream.

7 Then came in the magicians, the astrologers, the Chaldeans, and the soothsayers: and I told the dream before them; but they did not make known unto me the interpretation thereof.

DANIEL

8 -- But at the last Daniel came in before me, whose
name was Belteshazzar, according to the name of my
god, and in whom is the spirit of the holy gods: and
before him I told the dream, saying,

9 -- O Belteshazzar, master of the magicians, because
I know that the spirit of the holy gods is in thee, and
no secret troubleth thee, tell me the visions of my
dream that I have seen, and the interpretation
thereof.

10 -- Thus were the visions of mine head in my bed; I
saw, and behold a tree in the midst of the earth, and
the height thereof was great.

11 -- The tree grew, and was strong, and the height
thereof reached unto heaven, and the sight thereof to
the end of all the earth:

12 -- The leaves thereof were fair, and the fruit thereof
much, and in it was meat for all: the beasts of the field
had shadow under it, and the fowls of the heaven
dwelt in the boughs thereof, and all flesh was fed of it.

DANIEL

13 I saw in the visions of my head upon my bed, and, behold, a watcher and an holy one came down from heaven;

14 He cried aloud, and said thus, Hew down the tree, and cut off his branches, shake off his leaves, and scatter his fruit: let the beasts get away from under it, and the fowls from his branches:

15 Nevertheless leave the stump of his roots in the earth, even with a band of iron and brass, in the tender grass of the field; and let it be wet with the dew of heaven, and let his portion be with the beasts in the grass of the earth:

16 Let his heart be changed from man's, and let a beast's heart be given unto him; and let seven times pass over him.

17 This matter is by the decree of the watchers, and the demand by the word of the holy ones: to the intent that the living may know that the most High ruleth in the kingdom of men, and giveth it to whomsoever he will, and setteth up over it the basest of men.

DANIEL

18 This dream I king Nebuchadnezzar have seen. Now thou, O Belteshazzar, declare the interpretation thereof, forasmuch as all the wise men of my kingdom are not able to make known unto me the interpretation but thou art able; for the spirit of the holy gods is in thee.

19 Then Daniel, whose name was Belteshazzar, was astonied for one hour, and his thoughts troubled him. The king spake, and said, Belteshazzar, let not the dream, or the interpretation thereof, trouble thee. Belteshazzar answered and said, My lord, the dream be to them that hate thee, and the interpretation thereof to thine enemies.

20 The tree that thou sawest, which grew, and was strong, whose height reached unto the heaven, and the sight thereof to all the earth;

21 Whose leaves were fair, and the fruit thereof much, and in it was meat for all; under which the beasts of the field dwelt, and upon whose branches the fowls of the heaven had their habitation:

DANIEL

22 It is thou, O king, that art grown and become strong: for thy greatness is grown, and reacheth unto heaven, and thy dominion to the end of the earth.

23 And whereas the king saw a watcher and an holy one coming down from heaven, and saying, Hew the tree down, and destroy it; yet leave the stump of the roots thereof in the earth, even with a band of iron and brass, in the tender grass of the field; and let it be wet with the dew of heaven, and let his portion be with the beasts of the field, till seven times pass over him:

24 This is the interpretation, O king, and this is the decree of the most High, which is come upon my lord the king:

25 That they shall drive thee from men, and thy dwelling shall be with the beasts of the field, and they shall make thee to eat grass as oxen, and they shall wet thee with the dew of heaven, and seven times shall pass over thee, till thou know that the most High ruleth in the kingdom of men, and giveth it to whomsoever he will.

DANIEL

26 And whereas they commanded to leave the stump of the tree roots; thy kingdom shall be sure unto thee, after that thou shalt have known that the heavens do rule.

27 Wherefore, O king, let my counsel be acceptable unto thee, and break off thy sins by righteousness, and thine iniquities by shewing mercy to the poor; if it may be a lengthening of thy tranquillity.

28 All this came upon the king Nebuchadnezzar.

29 At the end of twelve months he walked in the palace of the kingdom of Babylon.

30 The king spake, and said, Is not this great Babylon, that I have built for the house of the kingdom by the might of my power, and for the honour of my majesty?

31 While the word was in the king's mouth, there fell a voice from heaven, saying, O king Nebuchadnezzar, to thee it is spoken; The kingdom is departed from thee.

DANIEL

32 And they shall drive thee from man, and thy dwelling shall be with the beasts of the field: they shall make thee to eat grass as oxen, and seven times shall pass over thee, until thou know that the most High ruleth in the kingdom of men, and giveth it to whomsoever he will.

33 The same hour was the thing fulfilled upon Nebuchadnezzar: and he was driven from men, and did eat grass as oxen, and his body was wet with the dew of heaven, till his hairs were grown like eagles' feathers, and his nails like birds' claws.

34 And at the end of the days I Nebuchadnezzar lifted up mine eyes unto heaven, and mine understanding returned unto me, and I blessed the most High, and I praised and honoured him that liveth for ever, whose dominion is an everlasting dominion, and his kingdom is from generation to generation:

DANIEL

35 And all the inhabitants of the earth are reputed as nothing: and he doeth according to his will in the army of heaven, and among the inhabitants of the earth: and none can stay his hand, or say unto him, What doest thou?

36 At the same time my reason returned unto me; and for the glory of my kingdom, mine honour and brightness returned unto me; and my counsellors and my lords sought unto me; and I was established in my kingdom, and excellent majesty was added unto me.

37 Now I Nebuchadnezzar praise and extol and honour the King of heaven, all whose works are truth, and his ways judgment: and those that walk in pride he is able to abase.

CHAPTER 5

1 Belshazzar the king made a great feast to a thousand of his lords, and drank wine before the thousand.

DANIEL

2 Belshazzar, whiles he tasted the wine, commanded to bring the golden and silver vessels which his father Nebuchadnezzar had taken out of the temple which was in Jerusalem; that the king, and his princes, his wives, and his concubines, might drink therein.

3 Then they brought the golden vessels that were taken out of the temple of the house of God which was at Jerusalem; and the king, and his princes, his wives, and his concubines, drank in them.

4 They drank wine, and praised the gods of gold, and of silver, of brass, of iron, of wood, and of stone.

5 In the same hour came forth fingers of a man's hand, and wrote over against the candlestick upon the plaister of the wall of the king's palace: and the king saw the part of the hand that wrote.

6 Then the king's countenance was changed, and his thoughts troubled him, so that the joints of his loins were loosed, and his knees smote one against another.

292

DANIEL

7 The king cried aloud to bring in the astrologers, the Chaldeans, and the soothsayers. And the king spake, and said to the wise men of Babylon, Whosoever shall read this writing, and shew me the interpretation thereof, shall be clothed with scarlet, and have a chain of gold about his neck, and shall be the third ruler in the kingdom.

8 Then came in all the king's wise men: but they could not read the writing, nor make known to the king the interpretation thereof.

9 Then was king Belshazzar greatly troubled, and his countenance was changed in him, and his lords were astonied.

10 Now the queen, by reason of the words of the king and his lords, came into the banquet house: and the queen spake and said, O king, live for ever: let not thy thoughts trouble thee, nor let thy countenance be changed.

DANIEL

1 There is a man in thy kingdom, in whom is the spirit of the holy gods; and in the days of thy father light and understanding and wisdom, like the wisdom of the gods, was found in him; whom the king Nebuchadnezzar thy father, the king, I say, thy father, made master of the magicians, astrologers, Chaldeans, and soothsayers;

2 Forasmuch as an excellent spirit, and knowledge, and understanding, interpreting of dreams, and shewing of hard sentences, and dissolving of doubts, were found in the same Daniel, whom the king named Belteshazzar: now let Daniel be called, and he will shew the interpretation.

3 Then was Daniel brought in before the king. And the king spake and said unto Daniel, Art thou that Daniel, which art of the children of the captivity of Judah, whom the king my father brought out of Jewry?

4 I have even heard of thee, that the spirit of the gods is in thee, and that light and understanding and excellent wisdom is found in thee.

DANIEL

15 And now the wise men, the astrologers, have been brought in before me, that they should read this writing, and make known unto me the interpretation thereof: but they could not shew the interpretation of the thing.

16 And I have heard of thee, that thou canst make interpretations, and dissolve doubts: now if thou canst read the writing, and make known to me the interpretation thereof, thou shalt be clothed with scarlet, and have a chain of gold about thy neck, and shalt be the third ruler in the kingdom.

17 Then Daniel answered and said before the king, Let thy gifts be to thyself, and give thy rewards to another; yet I will read the writing unto the king, and make known to him the interpretation.

18 O thou king, the most high God gave Nebuchadnezzar thy father a kingdom, and majesty, and glory, and honour:

DANIEL

19 And for the majesty that he gave him, all people, nations, and languages, trembled and feared before him: whom he would he slew; and whom he would he kept alive; and whom he would he set up; and whom he would he put down.

20 But when his heart was lifted up, and his mind hardened in pride, he was deposed from his kingly throne, and they took his glory from him:

21 And he was driven from the sons of men; and his heart was made like the beasts, and his dwelling was with the wild asses: they fed him with grass like oxen, and his body was wet with the dew of heaven; till he knew that the most high God ruled in the kingdom of men, and that he appointeth over it whomsoever he will.

22 And thou his son, O Belshazzar, hast not humbled thine heart, though thou knewest all this;

DANIEL

23 But hast lifted up thyself against the Lord of heaven; and they have brought the vessels of his house before thee, and thou, and thy lords, thy wives, and thy concubines, have drunk wine in them; and thou hast praised the gods of silver, and gold, of brass, iron, wood, and stone, which see not, nor hear, nor know: and the God in whose hand thy breath is, and whose are all thy ways, hast thou not glorified:

24 Then was the part of the hand sent from him; and this writing was written.

25 And this is the writing that was written, MENE, MENE, TEKEL, UPHARSIN.

26 This is the interpretation of the thing: MENE; God hath numbered thy kingdom, and finished it.

27 TEKEL; Thou art weighed in the balances, and art found wanting.

28 PERES; Thy kingdom is divided, and given to the Medes and Persians.

DANIEL

29 Then commanded Belshazzar, and they clothed Daniel with scarlet, and put a chain of gold about his neck, and made a proclamation concerning him, that he should be the third ruler in the kingdom.

30 In that night was Belshazzar the king of the Chaldeans slain.

31 And Darius the Median took the kingdom, being about threescore and two years old.

CHAPTER 6

1 It pleased Darius to set over the kingdom an hundred and twenty princes, which should be over the whole kingdom;

2 And over these three presidents; of whom Daniel was first: that the princes might give accounts unto them, and the king should have no damage.

3 Then this Daniel was preferred above the presidents and princes, because an excellent spirit was in him; and the king thought to set him over the whole realm.

DANIEL

4 Then the presidents and princes sought to find occasion against Daniel concerning the kingdom; but they could find none occasion nor fault; forasmuch as he was faithful, neither was there any error or fault found in him.

5 Then said these men, We shall not find any occasion against this Daniel, except we find it against him concerning the law of his God.

6 Then these presidents and princes assembled together to the king, and said thus unto him, King Darius, live for ever.

7 All the presidents of the kingdom, the governors, and the princes, the counsellors, and the captains, have consulted together to establish a royal statute, and to make a firm decree, that whosoever shall ask a petition of any God or man for thirty days, save of thee, O king, he shall be cast into the den of lions.

8 Now, O king, establish the decree, and sign the writing, that it be not changed, according to the law of the Medes and Persians, which altereth not.

DANIEL

9 Wherefore king Darius signed the writing and the decree.

10 Now when Daniel knew that the writing was signed, he went into his house; and his windows being open in his chamber toward Jerusalem, he kneeled upon his knees three times a day, and prayed, and gave thanks before his God, as he did aforetime.

11 Then these men assembled, and found Daniel praying and making supplication before his God.

12 Then they came near, and spake before the king concerning the king's decree; Hast thou not signed a decree, that every man that shall ask a petition of any God or man within thirty days, save of thee, O king, shall be cast into the den of lions? The king answered and said, The thing is true, according to the law of the Medes and Persians, which altereth not.

13 Then answered they and said before the king, That Daniel, which is of the children of the captivity of Judah, regardeth not thee, O king, nor the decree that thou hast signed, but maketh his petition three times a day.

DANIEL

14 Then the king, when he heard these words, was sore displeased with himself, and set his heart on Daniel to deliver him: and he laboured till the going down of the sun to deliver him.

15 Then these men assembled unto the king, and said unto the king, Know, O king, that the law of the Medes and Persians is, That no decree nor statute which the king establisheth may be changed.

16 Then the king commanded, and they brought Daniel, and cast him into the den of lions. Now the king spake and said unto Daniel, Thy God whom thou servest continually, he will deliver thee.

17 And a stone was brought, and laid upon the mouth of the den; and the king sealed it with his own signet, and with the signet of his lords; that the purpose might not be changed concerning Daniel.

18 Then the king went to his palace, and passed the night fasting: neither were instruments of musick brought before him: and his sleep went from him.

DANIEL

19 Then the king arose very early in the morning, and went in haste unto the den of lions.

20 And when he came to the den, he cried with a lamentable voice unto Daniel: and the king spake and said to Daniel, O Daniel, servant of the living God, is thy God, whom thou servest continually, able to deliver thee from the lions?

21 Then said Daniel unto the king, O king, live for ever.

22 My God hath sent his angel, and hath shut the lions' mouths, that they have not hurt me: forasmuch as before him innocency was found in me; and also before thee, O king, have I done no hurt.

23 Then was the king exceeding glad for him, and commanded that they should take Daniel up out of the den. So Daniel was taken up out of the den, and no manner of hurt was found upon him, because he believed in his God.

DANIEL

24   And the king commanded, and they brought those men which had accused Daniel, and they cast them into the den of lions, them, their children, and their wives; and the lions had the mastery of them, and brake all their bones in pieces or ever they came at the bottom of the den.

25   Then king Darius wrote unto all people, nations, and languages, that dwell in all the earth; Peace be multiplied unto you.

26   I make a decree, That in every dominion of my kingdom men tremble and fear before the God of Daniel: for he is the living God, and stedfast for ever, and his kingdom that which shall not be destroyed, and his dominion shall be even unto the end.

27   He delivereth and rescueth, and he worketh signs and wonders in heaven and in earth, who hath delivered Daniel from the power of the lions.

28   So this Daniel prospered in the reign of Darius, and in the reign of Cyrus the Persian.

DANIEL

CHAPTER 7

In the first year of Belshazzar king of Babylon Daniel had a dream and visions of his head upon his bed: then he wrote the dream, and told the sum of the matters.

2 Daniel spake and said, I saw in my vision by night, and behold, the four winds of the heaven strove upon the great sea.

3 And four great beasts came up from the sea, diverse one from another.

4 The first was like a lion, and had eagle's wings: I beheld till the wings thereof were plucked, and it was lifted up from the earth, and made stand upon the feet as a man, and a man's heart was given to it.

5 And behold another beast, a second, like to a bear, and it raised up itself on one side, and it had three ribs in the mouth of it between the teeth of it: and they said thus unto it, Arise, devour much flesh.

DANIEL

6. After this I beheld, and lo another, like a leopard, which had upon the back of it four wings of a fowl; the beast had also four heads; and dominion was given to it.

7. After this I saw in the night visions, and behold a fourth beast, dreadful and terrible, and strong exceedingly; and it had great iron teeth: it devoured and brake in pieces, and stamped the residue with the feet of it: and it was diverse from all the beasts that were before it; and it had ten horns.

8. I considered the horns, and, behold, there came up among them another little horn, before whom there were three of the first horns plucked up by the roots: and, behold, in this horn were eyes like the eyes of man, and a mouth speaking great things.

9. I beheld till the thrones were cast down, and the Ancient of days did sit, whose garment was white as snow, and the hair of his head like the pure wool: his throne was like the fiery flame, and his wheels as burning fire.

DANIEL

10 - A fiery stream issued and came forth from before him: thousand thousands ministered unto him, and ten thousand times ten thousand stood before him: the judgment was set, and the books were opened.

11 - I beheld then because of the voice of the great words which the horn spake: I beheld even till the beast was slain, and his body destroyed, and given to the burning flame.

12 - As concerning the rest of the beasts, they had their dominion taken away: yet their lives were prolonged for a season and time.

13 - I saw in the night visions, and behold, one like the Son of man came with the clouds of heaven, and came to the Ancient of days, and they brought him near before him.

14 - And there was given him dominion, and glory, and a kingdom, that all people, nations, and languages, should serve him: his dominion is an everlasting dominion, which shall not pass away, and his kingdom that which shall not be destroyed.

DANIEL

15 I Daniel was grieved in my spirit in the midst of my body, and the visions of my head troubled me.

16 I came near unto one of them that stood by, and asked him the truth of all this. So he told me, and made me know the interpretation of the things.

17 These great beasts, which are four, are four kings, which shall arise out of the earth.

18 But the saints of the most High shall take the kingdom, and possess the kingdom for ever, even for ever and ever.

19 Then I would know the truth of the fourth beast, which was diverse from all the others, exceeding dreadful, whose teeth were of iron, and his nails of brass; which devoured, brake in pieces, and stamped the residue with his feet;

20 And of the ten horns that were in his head, and of the other which came up, and before whom three fell; even of that horn that had eyes, and a mouth that spake very great things, whose look was more stout than his fellows.

DANIEL

21 I beheld, and the same horn made war with the
saints, and prevailed against them;

22 Until the Ancient of days came, and judgment
was given to the saints of the most High; and the time
came that the saints possessed the kingdom.

23 Thus he said, The fourth beast shall be the fourth
kingdom upon earth, which shall be diverse from all
kingdoms, and shall devour the whole earth, and shall
tread it down, and break it in pieces.

24 And the ten horns out of this kingdom are ten
kings that shall arise: and another shall rise after
them; and he shall be diverse from the first, and he
shall subdue three kings.

25 And he shall speak great words against the most
High, and shall wear out the saints of the most High,
and think to change times and laws: and they shall be
given into his hand until a time and times and the
dividing of time.

26 But the judgment shall sit, and they shall take
away his dominion, to consume and to destroy it unto
the end.

DANIEL

27 And the kingdom and dominion, and the greatness of the kingdom under the whole heaven, shall be given to the people of the saints of the most High, whose kingdom is an everlasting kingdom, and all dominions shall serve and obey him.

28 Hitherto is the end of the matter. As for me Daniel, my cogitations much troubled me, and my countenance changed in me: but I kept the matter in my heart.

CHAPTER 8

In the third year of the reign of king Belshazzar a vision appeared unto me, even unto me Daniel, after that which appeared unto me at the first.

2 And I saw in a vision, and it came to pass, when I saw, that I was at Shushan in the palace, which is in the province of Elam; and I saw in a vision, and I was by the river of Ulai.

DANIEL

3 Then I lifted up mine eyes, and saw, and behold, there stood before the river a ram which had two horns: and the two horns were high; but one was higher than the other, and the higher came up last.

4 I saw the ram pushing westward, and northward, and southward; so that no beasts might stand before him, neither was there any that could deliver out of his hand; but he did according to his will, and became great.

5 And as I was considering, behold, an he goat came from the west on the face of the whole earth, and touched not the ground: and the goat had a notable horn between his eyes.

6 And he came to the ram that had two horns, which I had seen standing before the river, and ran unto him in the fury of his power.

DANIEL

7 And I saw him come close unto the ram, and he was moved with choler against him, and smote the ram, and brake his two horns: and there was no power in the ram to stand before him, but he cast him down to the ground, and stamped upon him: and there was none that could deliver the ram out of his hand.

8 Therefore the he goat waxed very great: and when he was strong, the great horn was broken; and for it came up four notable ones toward the four winds of heaven.

9 And out of one of them came forth a little horn, which waxed exceeding great, toward the south, and toward the east, and toward the pleasant land.

10 And it waxed great, even to the host of heaven; and it cast down some of the host and of the stars to the ground, and stamped upon them.

11 Yea, he magnified himself even to the prince of the host, and by him the daily sacrifice was taken away, and the place of his sanctuary was cast down.

DANIEL

2 And an host was given him against the daily sacrifice by reason of transgression, and it cast down the truth to the ground, and it practised, and prospered.

3 Then I heard one saint speaking, and another saint said unto that certain saint which spake, How long shall be the vision concerning the daily sacrifice, and the transgression of desolation, to give both the sanctuary and the host to be trodden under foot?

4 And he said unto me, Unto two thousand and three hundred days; then shall the sanctuary be cleansed.

5 And it came to pass, when I, even I Daniel, had seen the vision, and sought for the meaning, then, behold, there stood before me as the appearance of a man.

6 And I heard a man's voice between the banks of Ulai, which called, and said, Gabriel, make this man to understand the vision.

DANIEL

17 So he came near where I stood: and when he came, I was afraid, and fell upon my face: but he said unto me, Understand, O son of man: for at the time of the end shall be the vision.

18 Now as he was speaking with me, I was in a deep sleep on my face toward the ground: but he touched me, and set me upright.

19 And he said, Behold, I will make thee know what shall be in the last end of the indignation: for at the time appointed the end shall be.

20 The ram which thou sawest having two horns are the kings of Media and Persia.

21 And the rough goat is the king of Grecia: and the great horn that is between his eyes is the first king.

22 Now that being broken, whereas four stood up for it, four kingdoms shall stand up out of the nation, but not in his power.

23 And in the latter time of their kingdom, when the transgressors are come to the full, a king of fierce countenance, and understanding dark sentences, shall stand up.

DANIEL

2-4- And his power shall be mighty, but not by his own power: and he shall destroy wonderfully, and shall prosper, and practise, and shall destroy the mighty and the holy people.

2-5- And through his policy also he shall cause craft to prosper in his hand; and he shall magnify himself in his heart, and by peace shall destroy many: he shall also stand up against the Prince of princes; but he shall be broken without hand.

2-6- And the vision of the evening and the morning which was told is true: wherefore shut thou up the vision; for it shall be for many days.

2-7- And I Daniel fainted, and was sick certain days: afterward I rose up, and did the king's business; and I was astonished at the vision, but none understood it.

DANIEL

CHAPTER 9

1 In the first year of Darius the son of Ahasuerus, of the seed of the Medes, which was made king over the realm of the Chaldeans;

2 In the first year of his reign I Daniel understood by books the number of the years, whereof the word of the LORD came to Jeremiah the prophet, that he would accomplish seventy years in the desolations of Jerusalem.

3 And I set my face unto the Lord God, to seek by prayer and supplications, with fasting, and sackcloth, and ashes:

4 And I prayed unto the LORD my God, and made my confession, and said, O Lord, the great and dreadful God, keeping the covenant and mercy to them that love him, and to them that keep his commandments;

5 We have sinned, and have committed iniquity, and have done wickedly, and have rebelled, even by departing from thy precepts and from thy judgments:

DANIEL

6 Neither have we hearkened unto thy servants the prophets, which spake in thy name to our kings, our princes, and our fathers, and to all the people of the land.

7 O Lord, righteousness belongeth unto thee, but unto us confusion of faces, as at this day; to the men of Judah, and to the inhabitants of Jerusalem, and unto all Israel, that are near, and that are far off, through all the countries whither thou hast driven them, because of their trespass that they have trespassed against thee.

8 O Lord, to us belongeth confusion of face, to our kings, to our princes, and to our fathers, because we have sinned against thee.

9 To the Lord our God belong mercies and forgivenesses, though we have rebelled against him;

10 Neither have we obeyed the voice of the LORD our God, to walk in his laws, which he set before us by his servants the prophets.

DANIEL

11 Yea, all Israel have transgressed thy law, even by departing, that they might not obey thy voice; therefore the curse is poured upon us, and the oath that is written in the law of Moses the servant of God, because we have sinned against him.

12 And he hath confirmed his words, which he spake against us, and against our judges that judged us, by bringing upon us a great evil: for under the whole heaven hath not been done as hath been done upon Jerusalem.

13 As it is written in the law of Moses, all this evil is come upon us: yet made we not our prayer before the LORD our God, that we might turn from our iniquities, and understand thy truth.

14 Therefore hath the LORD watched upon the evil, and brought it upon us: for the LORD our God is righteous in all his works which he doeth: for we obeyed not his voice.

DANIEL

5 And now, O Lord our God, that hast brought thy people forth out of the land of Egypt with a mighty hand, and hast gotten thee renown, as at this day; we have sinned, we have done wickedly.

6 O Lord, according to all thy righteousness, I beseech thee, let thine anger and thy fury be turned away from thy city Jerusalem, thy holy mountain: because for our sins, and for the iniquities of our fathers, Jerusalem and thy people are become a reproach to all that are about us.

7 Now therefore, O our God, hear the prayer of thy servant, and his supplications, and cause thy face to shine upon thy sanctuary that is desolate, for the Lord's sake.

8 O my God, incline thine ear, and hear; open thine eyes, and behold our desolations, and the city which is called by thy name: for we do not present our supplications before thee for our righteousnesses, but for thy great mercies.

DANIEL

19 O Lord, hear; O Lord, forgive; O Lord, hearken and do; defer not, for thine own sake, O my God: for thy city and thy people are called by thy name.

20 And whiles I was speaking, and praying, and confessing my sin and the sin of my people Israel, and presenting my supplication before the LORD my God for the holy mountain of my God;

21 Yea, whiles I was speaking in prayer, even the man Gabriel, whom I had seen in the vision at the beginning, being caused to fly swiftly, touched me about the time of the evening oblation.

22 And he informed me, and talked with me, and said, O Daniel, I am now come forth to give thee skill and understanding.

23 At the beginning of thy supplications the commandment came forth, and I am come to shew thee; for thou art greatly beloved: therefore understand the matter, and consider the vision.

DANIEL

24- Seventy weeks are determined upon thy people
and upon thy holy city, to finish the transgression,
and to make an end of sins, and to make reconciliation
for iniquity, and to bring in everlasting righteousness,
and to seal up the vision and prophecy, and to anoint
the most Holy.
25- Know therefore and understand, that from the
going forth of the commandment to restore and to
build Jerusalem unto the Messiah the Prince shall be
seven weeks, and threescore and two weeks: the
street shall be built again, and the wall, even in
troublous times.
26- And after threescore and two weeks shall
Messiah be cut off, but not for himself: and the people
of the prince that shall come shall destroy the city
and the sanctuary; and the end thereof shall be with
a flood, and unto the end of the war desolations are
determined.

DANIEL

27 And he shall confirm the covenant with many for one week: and in the midst of the week he shall cause the sacrifice and the oblation to cease, and for the overspreading of abominations he shall make it desolate, even until the consummation, and that determined shall be poured upon the desolate.

CHAPTER 10

In the third year of Cyrus king of Persia a thing was revealed unto Daniel, whose name was called Belteshazzar; and the thing was true, but the time appointed was long: and he understood the thing, and had understanding of the vision.

2 In those days I Daniel was mourning three full weeks.

3 I ate no pleasant bread, neither came flesh nor wine in my mouth, neither did I anoint myself at all, till three whole weeks were fulfilled.

4 And in the four and twentieth day of the first month, as I was by the side of the great river, which is Hiddekel;

DANIEL

5 Then I lifted up mine eyes, and looked, and behold a certain man clothed in linen, whose loins were girded with fine gold of Uphaz:

6 His body also was like the beryl, and his face as the appearance of lightning, and his eyes as lamps of fire, and his arms and his feet like in colour to polished brass, and the voice of his words like the voice of a multitude.

7 And I Daniel alone saw the vision: for the men that were with me saw not the vision; but a great quaking fell upon them, so that they fled to hide themselves.

8 Therefore I was left alone, and saw this great vision, and there remained no strength in me: for my comeliness was turned in me into corruption, and I retained no strength.

9 Yet heard I the voice of his words: and when I heard the voice of his words, then was I in a deep sleep on my face, and my face toward the ground.

10 And, behold, an hand touched me, which set me upon my knees and upon the palms of my hands.

DANIEL

11 And he said unto me, O Daniel, a man greatly beloved, understand the words that I speak unto thee, and stand upright: for unto thee am I now sent. And when he had spoken this word unto me, I stood trembling.

12 Then said he unto me, Fear not, Daniel: for from the first day that thou didst set thine heart to understand, and to chasten thyself before thy God, thy words were heard, and I am come for thy words.

13 But the prince of the kingdom of Persia withstood me one and twenty days: but, lo, Michael, one of the chief princes, came to help me; and I remained there with the kings of Persia.

14 Now I am come to make thee understand what shall befall thy people in the latter days: for yet the vision is for many days.

15 And when he had spoken such words unto me, I set my face toward the ground, and I became dumb.

DANIEL

16 And, behold, one like the similitude of the sons of man touched my lips: then I opened my mouth, and spake, and said unto him that stood before me, O my lord, by the vision my sorrows are turned upon me, and I have retained no strength.

17 For how can the servant of this my lord talk with this my lord? for as for me, straightway there remained no strength in me, neither is there breath left in me.

18 Then there came again and touched me one like the appearance of a man, and he strengthened me,

19 And said, O man greatly beloved, fear not: peace be unto thee, be strong, yea, be strong. And when he had spoken unto me, I was strengthened, and said, Let my lord speak; for thou hast strengthened me.

20 Then said he, Knowest thou wherefore I come unto thee? and now will I return to fight with the prince of Persia: and when I am gone forth, lo, the prince of Grecia shall come.

DANIEL

21 But I will shew thee that which is noted in the scripture of truth: and there is none that holdeth with me in these things, but Michael your prince.

CHAPTER 11

1 Also I in the first year of Darius the Mede, even I, stood to confirm and to strengthen him.

2 And now will I shew thee the truth. Behold, there shall stand up yet three kings in Persia; and the fourth shall be far richer than they all: and by his strength through his riches he shall stir up all against the realm of Grecia.

3 And a mighty king shall stand up, that shall rule with great dominion, and do according to his will.

4 And when he shall stand up, his kingdom shall be broken, and shall be divided toward the four winds of heaven; and not to his posterity, nor according to his dominion which he ruled: for his kingdom shall be plucked up, even for others beside those.

DANIEL

5 - And the king of the south shall be strong, and one
of his princes; and he shall be strong above him, and
have dominion; his dominion shall be a great dominion.
6 - And in the end of years they shall join themselves
together; for the king's daughter of the south shall
come to the king of the north to make an agreement:
but she shall not retain the power of the arm; neither
shall he stand, nor his arm: but she shall be given up,
and they that brought her, and he that begat her, and
he that strengthened her in these times.
7 - But out of a branch of her roots shall one stand up
in his estate, which shall come with an army, and shall
enter into the fortress of the king of the north, and
shall deal against them, and shall prevail:
8 - And shall also carry captives into Egypt their gods,
with their princes, and with their precious vessels of
silver and of gold; and he shall continue more years
than the king of the north.

DANIEL

9 So the king of the south shall come into his kingdom, and shall return into his own land.

10 But his sons shall be stirred up, and shall assemble a multitude of great forces: and one shall certainly come, and overflow, and pass through: then shall he return, and be stirred up, even to his fortress.

11 And the king of the south shall be moved with choler, and shall come forth and fight with him, even with the king of the north: and he shall set forth a great multitude; but the multitude shall be given into his hand.

12 And when he hath taken away the multitude, his heart shall be lifted up; and he shall cast down many ten thousands: but he shall not be strengthened by it.

13 For the king of the north shall return, and shall set forth a multitude greater than the former, and shall certainly come after certain years with a great army and with much riches.

DANIEL

14 And in those times there shall many stand up against the king of the south: also the robbers of thy people shall exalt themselves to establish the vision; but they shall fall.

15 So the king of the north shall come, and cast up a mount, and take the most fenced cities: and the arms of the south shall not withstand, neither his chosen people, neither shall there be any strength to withstand.

16 But he that cometh against him shall do according to his own will, and none shall stand before him: and he shall stand in the glorious land, which by his hand shall be consumed.

17 He shall also set his face to enter with the strength of his whole kingdom, and upright ones with him; thus shall he do: and he shall give him the daughter of women, corrupting her: but she shall not stand on his side, neither be for him.

DANIEL

18 - After this shall he turn his face unto the isles, and shall take many: but a prince for his own behalf shall cause the reproach offered by him to cease; without his own reproach he shall cause it to turn upon him.

19 - Then he shall turn his face toward the fort of his own land: but he shall stumble and fall, and not be found.

20 - Then shall stand up in his estate a raiser of taxes in the glory of the kingdom: but within few days he shall be destroyed, neither in anger, nor in battle.

21 - And in his estate shall stand up a vile person, to whom they shall not give the honour of the kingdom: but he shall come in peaceably, and obtain the kingdom by flatteries.

22 - And with the arms of a flood shall they be overthrown from before him, and shall be broken; yea, also the prince of the covenant.

DANIEL

23 And after the league made with him he shall work deceitfully: for he shall come up, and shall become strong with a small people.

24 He shall enter peaceably even upon the fattest places of the province; and he shall do that which his fathers have not done, nor his fathers' fathers; he shall scatter among them the prey, and spoil, and riches: yea, and he shall forecast his devices against the strong holds, even for a time.

25 And he shall stir up his power and his courage against the king of the south with a great army; and the king of the south shall be stirred up to battle with a very great and mighty army; but he shall not stand: for they shall forecast devices against him.

26 Yea, they that feed of the portion of his meat shall destroy him, and his army shall overflow: and many shall fall down slain.

27 And both these kings' hearts shall be to do mischief, and they shall speak lies at one table; but it shall not prosper: for yet the end shall be at the time appointed.

DANIEL

28 Then shall he return into his land with great riches; and his heart shall be against the holy covenant; and he shall do exploits, and return to his own land.

29 At the time appointed he shall return, and come toward the south; but it shall not be as the former, or as the latter.

30 For the ships of Chittim shall come against him: therefore he shall be grieved, and return, and have indignation against the holy covenant: so shall he do; he shall even return, and have intelligence with them that forsake the holy covenant.

31 And arms shall stand on his part, and they shall pollute the sanctuary of strength, and shall take away the daily sacrifice, and they shall place the abomination that maketh desolate.

32 And such as do wickedly against the covenant shall he corrupt by flatteries: but the people that do know their God shall be strong, and do exploits.

DANIEL

33 And they that understand among the people shall instruct many: yet they shall fall by the sword, and by flame, by captivity, and by spoil, many days.

34 Now when they shall fall, they shall be holpen with a little help: but many shall cleave to them with flatteries.

35 And some of them of understanding shall fall, to try them, and to purge, and to make them white, even to the time of the end: because it is yet for a time appointed.

36 And the king shall do according to his will; and he shall exalt himself, and magnify himself above every god, and shall speak marvellous things against the God of gods, and shall prosper till the indignation be accomplished: for that that is determined shall be done.

37 Neither shall he regard the God of his fathers, nor the desire of women, nor regard any god: for he shall magnify himself above all.

DANIEL

38 But in his estate shall he honour the God of forces: and a god whom his fathers knew not shall he honour with gold, and silver, and with precious stones, and pleasant things.

39 Thus shall he do in the most strong holds with a strange god, whom he shall acknowledge and increase with glory: and he shall cause them to rule over many, and shall divide the land for gain.

40 And at the time of the end shall the king of the south push at him: and the king of the north shall come against him like a whirlwind, with chariots, and with horsemen, and with many ships; and he shall enter into the countries, and shall overflow and pass over.

41 He shall enter also into the glorious land, and many countries shall be overthrown: but these shall escape out of his hand, even Edom, and Moab, and the chief of the children of Ammon.

42 He shall stretch forth his hand also upon the countries: and the land of Egypt shall not escape.

DANIEL

43 But he shall have power over the treasures of gold and of silver, and over all the precious things of Egypt: and the Libyans and the Ethiopians shall be at his steps.

44 But tidings out of the east and out of the north shall trouble him: therefore he shall go forth with great fury to destroy, and utterly to make away many.

45 And he shall plant the tabernacles of his palace between the seas in the glorious holy mountain; yet he shall come to his end, and none shall help him.

CHAPTER 12

1 And at that time shall Michael stand up, the great prince which standeth for the children of thy people: and there shall be a time of trouble, such as never was since there was a nation even to that same time: and at that time thy people shall be delivered, every one that shall be found written in the book.

2 And many of them that sleep in the dust of the earth shall awake, some to everlasting life, and some to shame and everlasting contempt.

DANIEL

3 And they that be wise shall shine as the brightness of the firmament; and they that turn many to righteousness as the stars for ever and ever.

4 But thou, O Daniel, shut up the words, and seal the book, even to the time of the end: many shall run to and fro, and knowledge shall be increased.

5 Then I Daniel looked, and, behold, there stood other two, the one on this side of the bank of the river, and the other on that side of the bank of the river.

6 And one said to the man clothed in linen, which was upon the waters of the river, How long shall it be to the end of these wonders?

7 And I heard the man clothed in linen, which was upon the waters of the river, when he held up his right hand and his left hand unto heaven, and sware by him that liveth for ever that it shall be for a time, times, and an half; and when he shall have accomplished to scatter the power of the holy people, all these things shall be finished.

DANIEL

8 And I heard, but I understood not: then said I, O my Lord, what shall be the end of these things?

9 And he said, Go thy way, Daniel: for the words are closed up and sealed till the time of the end.

10 Many shall be purified, and made white, and tried; but the wicked shall do wickedly: and none of the wicked shall understand; but the wise shall understand.

11 And from the time that the daily sacrifice shall be taken away, and the abomination that maketh desolate set up, there shall be a thousand two hundred and ninety days.

12 Blessed is he that waiteth, and cometh to the thousand three hundred and five and thirty days.

13 But go thou thy way till the end be: for thou shalt rest, and stand in thy lot at the end of the days.